a platter of figs
and other recipes

a platter of figs
and other recipes

david tanis

FOREWORD BY ALICE WATERS
PHOTOGRAPHS BY CHRISTOPHER HIRSHEIMER

Copyright © 2008 by David Tanis
Photographs copyright © 2008 by Christopher Hirsheimer

Published by Artisan
A Division of Workman Publishing Company, Inc.
225 Varick Street
New York, NY 10014-4381
www.artisanbooks.com

Library of Congress Cataloging-in-Publication Data

Tanis, David.
A platter of figs and other recipes / David Tanis.
p. cm
Includes bibliographical references and index.
ISBN: 978-1-57965-346-0 (alk. paper)
1. Cookery, International.   2. Menus.   3. Entertaining.   I. Title

TX725.A1T335 2008
641.59—dc22   2007049384

ISBN-13: 978-1-57965-301-9

Design by Jan Derevjanik
Printed in Singapore

10 9 8 7 6 5 4 3

Do you really need a recipe for a platter of figs? No. Is that the point? Yes. Does it have to be more complicated than that? Not really. Yet to serve the figs, you need to know about ripeness and seasonality—the seasons of the garden—and you need to know your figs. By this I mean, are they sun-ripened and bursting with jammy sweetness? Are they succulent enough to eat as is, or do they want a sprinkling of salt, a drizzle of good olive oil, perhaps a thin slice of prosciutto? A dab of fresh ricotta and honey to heighten the flavor? Or should you roast the figs with onions and thyme and serve them warm with rare-grilled duck breasts? This will determine their place in the menu—that is, as a first course, a main-course accompaniment, or a simple dessert.

The platter of figs perfectly illustrates the idea of eating with the seasons. Fresh figs are available for only a few weeks in the summer. The first figs are in June, but June figs usually pale in comparison to the late-summer crop, which benefits from warm August days. As with good tomatoes, you wait all year for the best figs to arrive. The reward is heavy, juicy fruit with oozing centers—sweet figs to swoon for. Above all, the platter of figs is a metaphor for the food I like. Fresh ripe figs are voluptuous and generous, luxurious and fleeting. And beautiful.

—DT

CONTENTS

FOREWORD by Alice Waters

There are two or three things I love about David Tanis that are not in this book. His hands, for one thing. There is a still picture on page 123, but when his hands are working, which is often, they are beautiful to watch: the fingers move with a practiced and graceful rhythm that reminds me of a great dancer at the bar. And I love David's habit of galvanizing himself by bursting into song in his big baritone. He has an impressive memory for words and music from a startlingly eclectic sampling of the twentieth-century songbook; and his delivery is . . . compelling.

What you will learn about David in this book is why he is one of the most important reasons our restaurant Chez Panisse remains a relevant enterprise well into the twenty-first century: He understands that creating a meal means creating your own reality, and he embodies that principle, week after week. We have always operated Chez Panisse on a rather archaic *table d'hôte* model: Every day we prepare and serve one menu, and one menu only, of three or four or five courses. The composition of a menu requires both tactical mastery and a well-tuned sense of taste; and its execution has to reconcile imagination with practicality. In these regards, David's menus are incomparable. Whatever the occasion, they all share a certain quality of harmonious simplicity uniquely his. And this book contains twenty-four of them, each a little masterpiece, and not least because not one of them requires heroic effort on the part of the partygiver.

When David started his career as chef at Chez Panisse, I asked him to make an impromptu lunch for me one day. It was that lunch's radical simplicity that won me over completely: He served me a piece of salmon on a little cutting board, with a bowl of salt alongside and a little lightly dressed pile of tiny greens. That was all. But it turned out to be exactly what I wanted. The salmon was exquisitely cooked; the greens were perfect. All the details were both intriguing and satisfying, with an underlying current of serious whimsy. For example, where had that board come from? We had plates, after all. Over the many years that have followed, David's sense of proportion and surprise has never failed him.

Now he has given us a very happy book, gloriously illustrated by Christopher Hirsheimer, who is just about the only food photographer I know who fully sees the beauty in simple food. And I can attest that David's food does, indeed, look—and taste—exactly as you would imagine from a close inspection of these images.

David's food reminds me so much of my ideal of what Chez Panisse should be, but this book is not a tribute to any restaurant or to any particular place and time—this book is really a love letter to you the reader, to whom David addresses himself with understanding, candor, and real wit. May you read it with pleasure!

A WAY TO EAT

This is a book about eating as much as it is about cooking. About eating with friends—and cooking for friends—and why that matters so much. Let me paint you a picture. The scene is Venice, Italy, in the autumn. The sun sets early in a gray sky. Bright orange persimmons hang on dark leafless branches. It's the cold-weather version of Venice, with rainy days and flooded walkways. (If this example sounds too rarified, imagine us in Baja, or Brooklyn.)

As it happens, it's Bob's birthday, which provides an excuse for a party. Instead of going to a restaurant, we'd rather cook together. Always. Of all the places we are staying, Alice's apartment has the best kitchen and biggest dining table, so we'll have dinner there. We rendezvous in the morning at the old, old market by the Rialto Bridge. As we stand upon a history of wet stone, the party has already begun.

Our favorite stop for espresso is tiny and outdoors, near the vegetable side of the market. You get a perfect coffee there, and a little panino of rucola and speck with a dab of garlicky pesto. It's necessary to fortify yourself before moving on.

The cheese shop next door, not much bigger and hospital clean, displays oils, egg pasta, and ravioli, but more to the point: real ricotta, spanking fresh mozzarella, irresistible pale white quivering cheeses. We don't resist. Our cheese is wrapped in paper, and we buy sliced prosciutto and mortadella, necessary for the aperitivo, hours hence.

Next, the vegetable stands—an autumn palette for the palate. Piles of green feathery fennel, purple grapes in boxes of straw, chicories in every color of burgundy. Honey-colored long-necked pears wrapped in pale tissue. Blushing pomegranates. Wild mushrooms, chestnuts. Now the fun starts in earnest. For me, this is the way the best meals begin: ogling vegetables, seeing what's at the market, what looks good, what feels right. Dinner for eight, maybe ten. Spur of the moment. Spread out and conquer.

Beneath the portico of the *pescheria,* the ancient fish market, miraculous creatures sparkle under bare bulbs. One lanky fishmonger is playing a rumba on the radio and dancing among the tuna and salt cod and the baskets of tiny live crabs. We see cuttlefish in every size from miniscule to giant, and wiggling gray shrimp from the lagoon. Another guy has the front half of a swordfish, including the sword. As soon as the marketing is finished, we schlep all our shopping bags to the nearby Cantina Do Mori, the best little wine bar in all Italy, for a stand-up glass of prosecco and a little prosciutto. Maybe a crostino of artichoke or porcini. Maybe another glass of something. Then we drag the shopping bags back to the refrigerator at Alice's place, and everyone goes their own way for the rest of the day.

We meet again at the cocktail hour—in the kitchen. Someone has brought flowers and candles. Someone else has popped around the corner to buy local wine straight from the spigot. Tonight's dinner for Bob: first, a frittura of tiny fish, quickly fried and devoured as we're peeling garlic, chopping parsley (and drinking prosecco). I make a Catalan *fideus* for the first course because I know Bob loves it—a spicy, saucy dish of noodles and shellfish that tastes of the sea. Then Tony's roast rabbit with porcini and Alice's salad of Treviso with fennel and anchovy dressing. Dessert is Randal's apple pie. And a platter of autumn fruits. We are at the table all night.

the case against restaurants

Yes, I'm a restaurant chef, and I do enjoy cooking for strangers, but I don't want to go to a restaurant on my days off. Okay, I'll admit to being slightly restaurant-phobic. I've always preferred to cook at home for friends. Cooking at home is a different experience entirely from the stressful world of restaurant cooking. To me, it doesn't feel like work. And even if it's not a perfect meal, the overriding mood of friends at the table still trumps a bad—or just okay—restaurant meal. Sound funny, coming from a chef?

We all long for a familial experience, even if it's not with our "real" family. The restaurants we love are those that make us feel as if we are part of a family. Of course, there are all kinds of good reasons to go to a restaurant: the rituals, the feeling of being spoiled, being waited on, being surprised. And, to be sure, there are all sorts of wonderful restaurants. I have my favorites. But a meal is an ethereal thing that requires a certain orchestration, and a lot of planets must be correctly aligned for it to succeed. The question is, will you be a happy captive with a positive experience or the unfortunate victim of a restaurant meal that has somehow gone very, very wrong?

Most restaurants are geared to serve only two or four at a time, six at most, and it is nice to dine *à deux,* or in an intimate foursome. But to get all the food up, ready, and cooked with care is difficult for most restaurants to pull off for a table of eight or ten. If there are more than six of you, stay home. It's more relaxed. It's cheaper. The schedule is flexible. You can have the table all night.

Who knows what they do back there in those restaurant kitchens? Then there's the harried waiter who is saddled with you, and vice versa. If I'm channeling a restaurant-wary grandmother for the moment, it's not so much fear of physical sickening as anxiety about what will arrive at the table. These days (now I really sound like a cranky old fart), so many restaurants are into the "wow!" factor. Eager ingredients-of-the-moment are doused with truffle oil (a synthetic product in vogue for all the wrong reasons), tasting menus offer an endless parade of clever food puns. I fret about salads: Will I get a decent one or something thrown together by a novice? Most restaurants mistakenly give the least-experienced cooks the job of dressing a salad, a skill that takes practice. The place is so crowded you can't hear a word, the décor is painfully trendy— or inauthentically old-time Euro. But what about the food? There's something really galling about going to a place that's supposed to be good and being served slapdash fare, or dolled up, manipulated architectural creations topped with foam. A bad meal can be so depressing.

We presume there's a chef back there in the kitchen somewhere, but more often than not there's a twenty-two-year-old culinary school graduate whose worldview, or whatever, is (understandably) undercultivated. I'd rather go to a diner and get a couple of eggs correctly fried than sample some chef's misguided fusion experiments. I'd rather go to a friend's house for dinner. But, really, I'd rather eat at home.

what makes a meal?

This book is a collection of menus: meals of simple food, simply served. I've observed that many people don't know how to make a menu, or how to design a meal. Most standard cookbooks list recipes by category: soup, salad, poultry, fish. What's often lacking is a way to think about them that turns them into a cohesive meal.

Simplicity is key. People who cook fussy food for their friends seem to have the least fun. I say leave that fussy food to those with a staff and a paid dishwasher. I've found that a three-course meal is the most doable—doable is everything—allowing the most pleasure for the cook as well as for his guests. As in music or poetry, a well-composed menu must have a pleasant sequence—something sprightly to begin, then a main course with more depth, and something refreshing to finish.

A meal needn't be fancy, nor should it take all day to make. But, that said, most of the menus in this book are not those 30-minute-specials-with-only-3-ingredients whose intent seems to be to keep you *out* of the kitchen. What's wrong with spending a little time in the kitchen? I like peeling the carrots, I like washing the lettuces. I like building a meal. I believe there's joy and amusement inherent in the cooking process, in putting the food into companionable serving vessels, in gathering in the kitchen and at the table, and in all the many little and big aesthetic decisions along the way.

How are we programmed to think about what we eat and what we want to eat? Society may have its ideas, but a thinking cook may want to decide for him/ herself. To my mind, the best menus are simply conceived, simply prepared, and simply served: a toast, a roast, a vegetable, a salad, cheese, fruit.

Start with a few slices of raw fennel and a plate of olives. Then bring me a beautiful bowl of steaming pasta with garlic and oil. For dessert, a just-ripe pear and some aged Parmigiano. There. A simple menu. Early autumn.

For breakfast, I don't crave pancakes, I want tomatoes and fresh white cheese splashed with olive oil. My preference is that of a salt-inclined palate over a sweet-craving one, but also one developed through reading, travel, and temperament. I do like a little something sweet after a meal, but I always prefer light, fresh, elemental, fruit-based desserts and that's what you'll find in this book.

who am I and how did I get this way?

What makes a boy from Ohio, born in the wrong century, raised on Tater Tots and Birds Eye, end up wanting to eat like a Greek peasant for breakfast, a French peasant for lunch, and a Moroccan peasant for dinner? Those who admire my cooking say I have a knack for making it all seem easy, that there's something about the way I serve food that is appealing, or exciting, or intriguing. How did this all begin?

Here is what I remember: I'm five years old, or a little younger. I awaken one early morning and determine to make breakfast for our little family. The sun has not yet risen. In the kitchen of our brick cookie-cutter, look-alike, two-bedroom cottage on Rutland Drive, on a mid-twentieth-century day, I set the table. It's a chrome-legged, speckled, and shiny red-top dinette table. My mother used to tell a story about my grandmother being born on a kitchen table in the olden days, and I imagine she was born on just such a table.

I put the spoons, the juice glasses, the folded paper napkins, the cereal bowls in their places. I put cereal in the bowls and pour on the milk. I fill the juice glasses. I toast the bread and spread the margarine. Everything is ready now, but no one is showing up. It must be early. It must be Sunday. I go back to bed. It is the first private kitchen moment I remember, and perhaps the first time I consciously prepared food for others.

Then I went underground. In my mother's world, children weren't really allowed in the kitchen. We had a housekeeper who was a very good cook and she, too, was strict about kitchen access. But sometimes she'd let us help her. When the grown-ups were away, I'd organize clandestine cooking forays for my siblings. My older sister did not have the knack, and my younger sister was too small. It was I who made the grilled bologna sandwiches, the popcorn, the James Cagney eggs.

I had already noticed that food at other people's houses was not like ours. Some houses had *real* butter. We were margarine-only, except for company. Company dinners (I soon learned to recognize my mother's six-dish company food repertoire) also featured cheese puffs and mixed nuts and brown-and-serve dinner rolls, spinach rice, lemon meringue pie. Weekday cooking was humble fare: beef brisket, broiled chicken thighs, meat loaf stretched with oatmeal, all invariably accompanied by a medley of frozen vegetables and some kind of starch, maybe noodle kugel. Salad was, of course, a wedge of iceberg. Exotic foods were found in other homes: Aunt Ruth made salad dressing from scratch, Aunt Edith cooked zucchini.

My adolescent undercover cooking led to experiments with baking. Teaching myself to make Cuban bread from the *New York Times*. And pies. In those days, I intended to be an artist, not a cook, but food and art were intertwined. I went everywhere with a sketch pad under my arm, and a few edibles in a knapsack. I would prepare private al fresco picnics. Those meals were my first still-life displays—an assortment of sardines, saltine crackers, tangerines, and cigarettes and magazines—first sketched in pen and ink, then photographed, then consumed.

At eighteen, I left home to go to a remote little college in the California desert, and to discover new foods. At school, I found myself more often in the kitchen than the library. While others were up late cramming for exams, I'd be in the pantry mixing up a big batch of dough. I began to bake bread in quantity. When the school hired a European chef for a semester, I gave up studying almost completely and made myself his apprentice. I learned how to make a proper omelette and how to butcher meat. But I was also out there training a mule to pull a wagon, experimenting with tanning hides and learning to grow vegetables. And there was still that canvas stretched in my room waiting for paint.

When I left school, still yearning for a rural experience and not ready for the real world by any means, I headed to the Pacific Northwest to join friends on a commune near Puget Sound. Called Cold Comfort Farm, after the 1930s novel, a British parody of farm life by Stella Gibbons, it was intended to be an artists' colony and self-sufficient. We milked a herd of goats and fattened two pigs named Ozzie and Harriet. We harvested everything in the garden and cooked dinner every night on an electric stove in an abandoned trailer. All around the farm, residents were constructing domes and teepees. The annual harvest ball was bacchanalian, an all-night feast under the stars.

Then I got on a Greyhound bus going south. A chef friend had asked me to join his team at a Southern California resort. I was barely twenty-one. With no restaurant experience at all, I was hired as pastry chef and handed index cards with the four recipes I would need. I was expected to use up all the cake mixes left behind by the previous regime. That was fine with me. The Chalet, with waitresses in skimpy red dirndls, served "continental food" like veal Oscar. We were all let go at the end of the season, but by then I was hooked.

I hitchhiked to San Francisco to try my luck at faking my way into another restaurant. It was a heady time (a loaded phrase). All around me, people were dropping out of school to pursue dreams. Being a chef was not on the list of acceptable professions for a nice boy from Dayton, Ohio, but what did I care?

Chez Panisse had just opened. It seemed to me a fantasy world, peopled by the coolest folks. I had a friend who cooked there. Aside from letting me work an occasional prep or dishwashing shift, Alice paid me little attention. But, still, I hung around. The whole place felt Euro and special. There were parties nearly every night. From time to time, I would ask Alice for a job, but she always seemed not to hear. I took jobs in kitchens around the Bay Area. When I applied for work (I looked a bit Rasputin-like in those days) at the Bay Wolf restaurant in Oakland, Michael Wild, the chef, looked at me and said, "So, what are you, a poet?" "Not really," said I, "but I like to cook." He gave me two dishwashing shifts and three nights steaming vegetables. When he found out I really could cook, he gave me carte blanche.

Finally, the Chez Panisse bread baker left to marry and take a honeymoon. I covered his shifts and got more than a big toe in the door. Soon I was making pizzas and salads. One day, Alice hired me to run the café upstairs, the ultimate learn-on-the-job opportunity, exciting but intimidating. I submitted menus weekly for scrutiny, and Alice watched over me as I figured out how to be chef and manager. She would come up and taste the food before lunch, offer feedback freely, then race off. If other restaurants were dog-and-pony shows, this one was a three-ring circus. Two restaurants in one. Cooks came and went, everyone had a personality (some had two), lunch was busy, dinner was busier. Bastille Day, New Year's Eve.

Tom Guernesey, the exuberant maitre d', would breeze through the kitchen and cackle. Peggy Smith, already a cowgirl at heart, wore pointy-toed boots and played Dolly Parton full blast while chopping parsley with two big knives at rapid-fire pace. Paul Bertolli was the chef downstairs, and he was so tall they had to raise the vent above the stove so he wouldn't bump his head. Paul was in a period of inspired creativity, making beautiful food. He always seemed serene and in control, while I was flying by the seat of my pants. Eventually I found my groove, and seven years passed quickly. I would happily have continued. Chez Panisse is a restaurant like no other. You're spoiled by its particular combination of purity and chaos and can't work anywhere else unless you open your own place. In the early 1990s, such an opportunity arose for me in Santa Fe.

When I moved to Santa Fe, everyone was doing either traditional Southwest menus (green chile stew, pozole, pupusas, sopaipillas, carne adovada) or New Wave, squirt-bottle East-meets-Southwest fusion (black bean wontons with jicama-habanero crema and mango-ginger dipping sauce—that sort of thing). The prevailing idea was that any hot chile dish, wherever it came from, could find a home—and perhaps an unusual partner—on a Santa Fe menu.

Mark Miller was way out in front at Coyote Café doing glitzy neo-Southwestern cowboy cuisine. Up the street, Katherine Kagel was serving *huevos motuleños* and café au lait for breakfast at Pasqual's, with a line around the block. Our idea at Café Escalera was to do a San Francisco Bay Area–style restaurant based on fresh ingredients. When people asked what sort of restaurant we were, we would say, "Mediterranean-inspired, market-driven, simple seasonal cooking." The response was usually, "So what is it, French, Italian?" We'd say our menu changed daily, "based on the availability of the best . . ." "Oh," they'd reply. "We were looking for Southwestern—do you have pasta?"

Still, we persevered. During the short growing season—it could snow in June and we could have first frost by September—we bought all our fresh produce from local farmers. We became known as a place you could get a good salad or a properly grilled piece of fish. We even baked our own bread. We made mayonnaise by hand, got famous for our skinny pommes frites. The menu was small, and we really did change it every day, twice a day. Business was another story. Santa Fe was in a descent from the boom of the late eighties. Something called the hantavirus scared off tourists for a while. And we were one of more than two hundred restaurants in a very small town.

We were always full for lunch, and we turned people away in June and July, but there were many winter nights when we simply sent staff home. We were voted Best Restaurant in New Mexico by Zagat, our wine list won awards. But the gods had decided otherwise, and finally the place closed.

I returned home. To Chez Panisse. Alice found plenty for me to do—working on the *Chez Panisse Café Cookbook,* catering, filling in for cooks on holiday. I began sharing the downstairs restaurant chef job with long-time chef Jean-Pierre Moullé. We would split the week, each running the kitchen half-time. All was well until 2001, when I made a whimsical, spur-of-the-moment decision to move to Paris. (Jean-Pierre was inclined to spend long summers at his house in Bordeaux.) What to do? Alice, ever practical, ever unconventional, proposed the perfect solution: divide the year, not the week. We could each work six months straight, full-time, then have six months to recover, replenish, return to Paris, go off to Buenos Aires, whatever. We both agreed it was a lovely plan. Evidently, you *can* go home again.

the job of the cookbook

What can you learn from this book? That a party can be any gathering of eaters at a table. That a fine meal doesn't have to necessarily be elaborate. That the best meals mirror nature and celebrate the seasonal.

The idea that we enjoy the summer's harvest and preserve what we can for the winter is an old notion. Even though global marketing and modern refrigeration have paved over much of this territory, there is a movement now toward a more seasonal life, and I consider myself part of it. A good cook knows the pleasure of a seasonal kitchen. Eating seasonally is eating sustainably, supporting local farmers, and preserving the land, but it has everything to do with pleasure as well. There's no denying the flavor of a good tomato picked ripe or a cucumber straight from the garden or a new-crop apple. The experience is pure and sensual.

serving food: pretty versus beautiful

Generally I don't like pretty food, but I am in awe of beautiful food. Here's what I mean: I think food should look natural, not contrived. Plums in a bowl are nothing more than a repetition of shapes: what could be more beautiful? Tender green beans—briefly cooked, dressed with oil, and gently piled on a platter—are beautiful in a way that stacked, squeezed, decorated, gussied-up creations will never be. Simple well-worn earthen cooking vessels, cazuelas, gratin dishes, deep bowls, terrines—all enhance the simple glory of the food itself. Platters speak of abundance and generosity. There's a communal aspect to a platter as well: It must be passed from diner to diner. It must be shared.

Now, about cooking for friends. At my house there always seem to be at least eight of them and I've designed all the menus in this book for a table of eight or ten. That should not be daunting. And most recipes can be easily halved, or increased (as in add another potato to the pot). What matters is that you do it.

spring menus

favas and other harbingers

Fava Bean Salad with Mountain Ham and Mint

Roasted Veal with Morel Mushrooms and Saffron Carrots

Hazelnut Sponge Cake

So strange, isn't it, the power of food memories. A simple salad of fava beans is always magical and exciting to me. I first encountered it in Spain, in a well-known Catalan restaurant not far from the Dalí Museum. I had barely taken my seat when a torrential rainstorm put out the power in the entire village of Figueres. Sitting in the blacked-out restaurant seemed appropriately Dalíesque. My day had already been slightly surreal. I'd traveled to Figueres in a ghostly empty third-class train with dusty red-velvet seats and tattered lace curtains. There were no other passengers, nor did I see a conductor. I wondered if there was even a driver. I spent the day among Dalí's giant eyeballs, bizarre dioramas, and weird self-portraits. Now the artist seemed to be orchestrating my dinner with thunder and lightning—his kind of drama. The waiters calmly went about lighting lanterns and candles, and the place became eerily, wonderfully quiet, without the hum of generators or any equipment. When it was set before me by candlelight, that simple bean salad—a combination of favas, mint, good olive oil, and excellent Spanish ham—symbolized the whole experience. It still does.

Fava Bean Salad with Mountain Ham and Mint

If fava beans are in the market, you know it's spring, or spring somewhere nearby. Their giant green pods look like something strange and juicy, perhaps from another planet. In fact, they are the original Mediterranean bean. Early favas are small and tender; they get starchier as the season progresses. Favas are more than a little fussy to peel, but peel you must to appreciate them fully. Fresh fava beans are so good, though, they are worth the effort.

I usually try to enlist help and I always wish I had a houseful of kids or a couple of resident grandmothers . . . peeling favas makes a nice multigenerational chore. For this salad, the fava beans are removed from the pods, cooked briefly, peeled, and combined with thinly sliced raw fennel (or you could use raw artichokes or asparagus).

8 to 10 pounds fresh young fava beans
   in the pod (10 pounds will yield
   about 6 cups beans)
3 or 4 fennel bulbs, about 2 pounds
1 bunch scallions, thinly slivered
Salt and pepper

Fruity olive oil
1 bunch mint
1 lemon
12 slices cured ham, such as jamón
   serrano or prosciutto
Arugula leaves (optional)

Shuck the fava beans from their pods. To remove their skins, blanch the beans in boiling water for 10 seconds, then cool in a large basin of ice water. Pop out the beans, piercing the gray-green skin with your thumbnail to free the bright green, barely cooked bean. Cover the favas with a damp towel.

Trim and wash the fennel.

When you are ready to make the salad, slice the fennel into thin shreds (a mandoline works well for this) and put them in a bowl. Add the fava beans, scallions, and a good sprinkling of sea salt. Drizzle generously with fruity olive oil to coat. Coarsely chop the mint leaves and add them, then squeeze the juice of half the lemon over the salad. Toss well with your hands, then taste and correct with salt, oil, and/or lemon juice.

Pile the salad onto a large platter, add a few grinds of black pepper, and surround with thin slices of mountain ham, such as jamón serrano or prosciutto. Or julienne or tear the ham into strips and scatter over the salad. Garnish with a few arugula leaves if you like, and serve immediately. *serves 8–10*

{VARIATION} FAVA BEAN MASH ON TOAST

If the favas you find are larger and starchier, make a savory fava bean spread. Just buy a few pounds, and stew the peeled beans in ¼ cup olive oil with a little chopped garlic, a few whole cumin seeds, salt, and pepper. Add a glass of water and simmer for about 10 minutes, until soupy. Mash the beans with a wooden spoon, then spread on garlic toast (see page 182).

Olive oil was never a fancy ingredient in the Mediterranean.
Still isn't. You just used what you had, and there were olive trees aplenty on those
sunny hillsides. And it wasn't the only oil: grapeseed, rapeseed, poppy seed, cot-
tonseed, and other nut oils like walnut or hazelnut were used frequently too, there
and in other regions. So it's pretty astounding to see today's fetishizing of olive
oil—marketing high-priced boutique oils to a foodie crowd.

Olive oil *is* a delicious, healthy oil to cook with. It's the logical, natural oil to
use when cooking Mediterranean food, and almost any midpriced oil produces
good results. There are certainly some exquisite oils that do make a difference to
food, such as a peppery Tuscan oil, or a sweet, round French oil from Provence—
especially when you're not cooking with it. Use these oils as a final drizzle on a
dish or for dressing the simplest green salad. But you don't need a $30 bottle to
make good food.

The supermarket, unfortunately, is not usually the best place to buy olive oil,
because even if it's labeled extra virgin, it may have been on the shelves too long,
or it may not be a good brand to begin with. Health food stores quite often sell
decent olive oils in bulk that come from Spain, Turkey, or Greece, even California.
For everyday cooking, these can be pleasantly fruity and flavorful.

Provençal housewives have a trick I like for stretching their olive oil: they mix
it half-and-half with vegetable oil and keep it in a wine bottle by the side of the
stove. They use that mix for everyday sautéing and frying. In this economizing
gesture, the flavor of the olive oil still comes through.

Having said all that, you still have to look for extra virgin oil, because the
term means the oil has not been heated or processed in any fashion. So-called pure
olive oil is a misnomer; it is made after the first pressing of olives, from the dregs,
which are heated, then centrifuged and blended with additives. Don't buy it.

Roasted Veal with Morel Mushrooms and Saffron Carrots

Factory-style veal—the result of a giant dairy industry gone amok, with cast-off male calves subjected to inhumane treatment—has animal rights people up in arms, and rightly so. Happily, wholesome, natural milk-fed veal is being raised again, and its flavor is excellent. If you can't find good veal, use a pork loin roast (from a politically correct nonfactory pig farm).

Wild morel mushrooms are another delicacy, abundant in the spring woods and fun to hunt, but they're are also relatively easy to find at good produce markets, for a price. Their flavor is deeper than that of other wild mushrooms. (In a pinch, dried morels, which rehydrate well, are an acceptably good substitute, or use a combination of fresh button mushrooms and dried morels.) Morels need to be cooked longer than other mushrooms to bring out their flavor and create a rich-tasting sauce. In other seasons, you can use chanterelles or porcini.

1 boneless shoulder roast of veal,
   4 to 5 pounds
Salt and pepper
6 garlic cloves, sliced
Olive oil
A few rosemary sprigs
A few thyme sprigs
6 ounces thinly sliced pancetta
1 pound morel mushrooms

2 tablespoons butter
2 shallots, finely chopped
2 cups Dark Chicken Stock
   (recipe follows)
Water or dry white wine
½ cup Crème Fraîche (page 41)
   or heavy cream
Saffron Carrots (recipe follows)

Season the roast well with salt and pepper. Insert the garlic slices in the loose flesh on the underside of the roast. Drizzle a little olive oil over the meat. Roughly chop the rosemary and thyme sprigs and press them all over the meat. Wrap the pancetta strips around the roast and place in a roasting pan. Refrigerate for a couple of hours, or overnight.

Bring the meat to room temperature, and preheat the oven to 400°F. Roast the veal for 45 minutes to an hour, until the internal temperature is 130°F. Let the meat rest on a platter, loosely covered, for at least 15 minutes before carving.

While the meat is cooking, prepare the sauce. Over high heat, reduce the dark chicken stock by half to yield one cup. Set aside. Swish the mushrooms quickly in a large bowl of warm water—morels can be sandy—then lift them out to a colander. Blot the mushrooms with a towel, and trim and discard the tough stems. Coarsely chop the morels or, if they are small, cut them in half.

Melt the butter in a saucepan. Slowly sauté the shallots in the butter, stirring occasionally, until lightly browned. Turn up the heat and add the mushrooms, salt, and pepper. Stew the mushrooms with the shallots for a minute or two, then add the reduced stock. Simmer gently for 10 to 15 minutes.

When the roast is out of the oven and resting, pour off the fat from the roasting pan. Add a little water or white wine and scrape up the roasty bits from the bottom of the pan. Add these pan juices to the sauce, then stir in the crème fraîche and simmer the sauce for 10 minutes more.

Slice the meat, arrange it on a platter, and spoon over the mushroom sauce. Serve the saffron carrots separately. *serves 8–10*

dark chicken stock

To make an unctuous dark sauce to serve with a roast, begin with a dark stock. It takes a little time to make, but it's wonderful to have on hand in the freezer.

1 organic chicken, about 4 pounds	6 quarts water
1 medium onion, quartered	A thyme branch
2 medium carrots, peeled and chunked	Half a bay leaf
1 celery stalk	1 tablespoon tomato paste

Preheat the oven to 400°F. Split the chicken in half. Place it, unseasoned, in a shallow roasting pan and scatter the vegetables over and around it. Roast uncovered for an hour or so, starting at 400°F, then, after about 15 minutes, lower the heat to 350°F, turning the chicken over now and then. The idea is to get everything as darkly browned and caramelized as possible without burning it. The chicken, of course, will be quite overcooked.

Put the contents of the roasting pan in a stockpot and cover with the water. Add the thyme branch and bay leaf half. Bring to a boil, skimming off the froth, then reduce to a simmer.

Meanwhile, deglaze the roasting pan with a little hot water, scraping it with a wooden spoon; take care to dissolve all the brown bits in the pan. Add the tomato paste and stir it into the juices. Pour the dissolved juices into the stockpot.

Simmer the stock for 2 hours, or until reduced by half. Strain, refrigerate, and then degrease. The stock will have jelled slightly, and it should be a rich brown. It can be refrigerated for several days or frozen for future use.

For a simple dark sauce reduction, boil 2 cups of the half-reduced stock until 1 cup remains. Just 1 cup of this second reduction will be so rich it will make enough sauce for 8 servings.

saffron carrots

It's amazing how a little saffron and garlic can transform ordinary carrots into something sublime.

Peel 3 pounds carrots and slice into thin coins. Cook in 2 tablespoons butter with a little crumbled saffron and a couple chopped garlic cloves. Season well with salt and pepper and a scant teaspoon of freshly grated lemon zest. Add a cup of water and simmer, covered, for 5 minutes, or until the carrots are tender.

{CARROTS, ANOTHER WAY} MASHED POTATOES
WITH CARROTS AND SAFFRON

Boil 2 pounds potatoes and 2 pounds carrots in salted water until tender. Drain and add a little crumbled saffron, butter, and grated lemon zest. Mash the potatoes and carrots and thin with a little milk or Crème Fraîche (page 41).

Hazelnut Sponge Cake

I'm not much for rich, gooey cakes, but this one is neither. A small slice is especially good with a little fresh fruit and a spoonful of Barely Whipped Cream (page 69). It's nice, too, frosted with a layer of coffee-flavored whipped cream, or used as a base for tiramisu. The cake keeps well and can be made a day or two ahead.

1 pound shelled hazelnuts

8 large eggs, separated

¾ cup sugar

Grated zest and juice of 1 lemon

2 tablespoons cake flour, matzo meal, or dry bread crumbs

½ teaspoon salt

Preheat the oven to 400°F. Line a 10-inch springform pan with a round of parchment paper (or butter and flour the pan) and set aside. Roast the hazelnuts on a baking sheet for 10 minutes, or until the skins blister and the nuts are lightly toasted. Put the roasted nuts in a dry dish towel and rub them together to remove the blistered skins. When the hazelnuts are cool, coarsely chop in a food processor or with a nut grinder.

In a mixing bowl, beat the egg yolks with the sugar until creamy. Add the lemon zest, lemon juice, flour, salt, and chopped nuts and mix well. Whip the egg whites until stiff. Stir one-third of the whites into the batter to lighten it, then gently fold in the rest of the whites.

Scrape the batter into the cake pan and bake for 15 minutes at 350°F. Turn the oven down to 325°F and bake until a skewer inserted into the center of the cake comes out clean, about 25 to 30 minutes more. Let the cake cool completely on a rack before unmolding.

how to cook a rabbit

Spinach Cake with Herb Salad

Mustard Rabbit in the Oven

Parsnips Epiphany-Style

Apple Tart

Rabbits are hideously misunderstood in this country, except by a few of us quiet loyalists who persist in our devotion. Every chef I know has a story about trying to put rabbit on the menu—not a good idea for the Easter crowd—and a few brave chefs do prevail. In Europe, rabbits are common in markets and on menus, but it seems Americans would still rather pet them than eat them. Yet rabbits were once popular fare in this country. And farm-raised rabbit is the very model of a perfect meat: mild and sweet, tender and quite lean, high in protein. Rabbits' all-vegetable diet makes them a very healthy thing to eat.

On the other hand, rabbit *recipes* abound. And fresh rabbit is rather easily found—it's encouraging that a Google search for "farm-raised rabbit" yields ever more sources—though it may mean ordering ahead from a good Italian butcher, or finding a Latino meat market. Some supermarkets stock rabbit "fryers." It is worth investigating the rabbit underground in your area.

The old joke, in this case, is true: just about anything you can do with a chicken, you can do with a rabbit. Once you are a rabbit fan, you'll choose the part

you like best. The belly flap is very good, as are the forelegs, saddle, neck, even the head. The hind legs are fine if they're roasted perfectly, but better if braised a little longer. Rabbit liver is delicious sautéed rareish, seasoned with nothing more than salt, pepper, and olive oil. Slice it, still warm, and serve on toast as an hors d'oeuvre with drinks, or as a treat for the cook. Rabbit kidneys, likewise, are succulent and mild, not at all strong tasting. At our table, we fight over the kidneys. Rabbit makes a tasty broth too. As cooks and diners become more adventurous, let's hope for a rabbit revival, and maybe even a rabbit in every pot.

Spinach Cake with Herb Salad

This cake—a cross between a custard and a frittata—tastes best at room temperature, so it's best made several hours ahead of time. It's great on a picnic, or as part of a cold lunch. It can be made with other greens, such as chard, mustard or turnip greens, or nettles. Made with spinach, the cake is a brilliant green, its flavor deeply satisfying.

2 bunches spinach, about 2 pounds

2 medium leeks

2 tablespoons butter

Salt and pepper

Nutmeg

2 cups whole milk

6 large eggs

Pinch of cayenne

A little Parmigiano

Herb Salad (recipe follows)

Cut the spinach into 1-inch-wide ribbons, discarding any tough stems. Swish the greens in a large basin of cold water, then lift them out to a colander. Repeat the process 2 more times, with fresh water each time. It is tempting but unwise to stop after 2 washings. After the third washing, you shouldn't see any sand or grit in the water.

Trim the leeks and peel off the tough outer layer. Cut the leeks into small dice. Fill a bowl with warm tap water and add the leeks. Agitate the leeks with your hand. Let the dirt and sand settle in the bowl, then scoop the leeks from the water. Repeat the process 2 more times.

Melt the butter in a deep, heavy-bottomed pan over medium heat. Add the leeks, season with salt and pepper, and sauté, stirring occasionally, until they are tender but still green, about 5 minutes.

Turn up the heat and scrape a little nutmeg over the leeks. Now add the drained spinach in layers, sprinkling each layer with a little salt. Cover tightly, and let the spinach steam rapidly over the leeks, removing the lid to stir once or twice. (The water clinging to the spinach will provide enough moisture for steaming.) When the spinach is just barely wilted, 2 minutes or less, turn out the contents of the pot onto a platter and let cool. Be sure to save any cooking juices that have accumulated.

Preheat the oven to 400°F. When the spinach-leek mixture is cool, taste for seasoning and adjust—it should be highly seasoned. In a blender or food processor, puree the cooked vegetables with the milk and eggs in batches, adding a little more salt, pepper, and a pinch of cayenne. Add any remaining cooking juices to one of the batches and whiz again.

Pour the soupy green batter into a buttered baking dish or a 9- or 10-inch deep-dish pie pan. Grate a scant 2 tablespoons Parmigiano over the top, and bake uncovered for 45 minutes, or until a knife inserted in the center comes out clean. Cool to room temperature. Cut into wedges and serve with the herb salad.

herb salad

A salad of tiny lettuces and sweet herbs is a surprising and delicate thing. It must be dressed at the very last moment, with a very light hand. Use many different kinds of leaves; avoid anything too spicy or strong. Let the flavor of the herbs dominate. Belgian endive adds crunch and volume; so do mild watercress leaves and thinly sliced radish or young fennel. Garnish the plates with Soft-Center Hard-Cooked Eggs (page 154), if you like.

8 handfuls small arugula and lettuce
   leaves, the smaller the better,
   about ¾ pound
4 Belgian endive (optional)
Chervil, parsley, basil, mint, and
   tarragon sprigs plus a few celery
   leaves from the center of the bunch

1 shallot, finely diced
Juice of ½ lemon, or a little more
Salt and pepper
¼ cup olive oil

Wash and gently dry the arugula and lettuce leaves. Trim the endive, if using; discard the outer leaves, and slice crosswise about 1 inch thick. Combine with the washed greens and wrap in a clean towel and refrigerate until ready to serve.

Pluck the herb leaves from their stems, tearing larger leaves into rough ribbons. You will need roughly 2 cups of a mixture of sweet herbs, plus a few chopped celery leaves.

Prepare a vinaigrette: Macerate the shallot with the lemon juice and a little salt. Then whisk in the olive oil. Add a little freshly ground pepper.

Put the arugula, lettuce, and herb leaves in a low wide bowl. Sprinkle very lightly with salt and toss gently. Rewhisk the dressing and spoon half of it over the salad, then toss again to coat very lightly. The idea is that the salad will be barely dressed, but sprightly. Adjust with a little more vinaigrette, lemon juice, or a drop of oil. Toss, taste, and serve. (A spoonful of vinaigrette over the spinach cake tastes good too.)

If you have a garden, there's nothing more satisfying than picking salad just before dinner: you can't find a fresher salad—the greens taste alive. For those of us without gardens, our goal is to approximate the garden salad, relying on the efforts of good greengrocers and farm stands.

With greens, it's buyer beware. You may be tempted by premixed salad, in bags or bins, but how fresh can these greens really be? It is better to buy individual lettuces, large or small, and mix your own. Try for a variety of flavors and textures, but make it mostly lettuces. I generally find beet greens, mustard greens, and the like too strong, but many commercial growers market these "sturdier" salad mixes, probably because they have a longer shelf life. They are sometimes called "spring mix," but to me these leaves are better softened in a stir-fry. Likewise, the spicy "mesclun mix" in the States has nothing do with the French original, which in France usually means young lettuce shoots of different varieties mixed with a bit of arugula and chervil. All the seeds are sown together, then cut with scissors as they reach the proper size.

For me, a classic mixed green salad needs a combination of tender red and green oak-leaf lettuces, curly or Belgian endive, a little mild arugula or watercress, some small romaine leaves, butter or Bibb lettuce, and perhaps some flat-leaf parsley leaves pulled from the stem.

When buying lettuce, size is not as important as freshness. The lettuce should look sassy and tantalizing, the stem ends freshly cut. You must always refuse wilted or droopy heads; I find they can bring on a kind of cook's melancholia or in some cases, severe depression. Pursue perky, frisky greens—they're a cheap thrill.

To wash lettuces, fill a large basin with cold water. Pluck off any tough outer leaves, then separate the inner leaves and plunge them into the water. Inspect arugula or watercress for tough stems and trim them. Swish the lettuces with your hands and gently agitate to allow sand and soil to sink to the bottom of the basin. Try not to keep the greens in water for more than 5 minutes, or they'll get waterlogged. Lift the greens from the basin to a colander. Give the colander a shake and let the lettuces drain. To dry the greens, lay them on kitchen towels, stacked in layers, then roll up into a loose log and refrigerate.

An old-fashioned drying trick is the pillowcase method, where drained salad greens are stuffed into a pillowcase, shaken and fluffed gently, then rolled up. The French are fond of the human centrifuge technique, where wet lettuces are put in a wire basket, carried outdoors, held at arm's length, and spun rapidly, like a pitcher winding up for a fastball. If you like those little drawstring salad spinners that seem to be de rigueur in the modern kitchen, I won't hold it against you, but I have become disenchanted with them. Why? Because that puts just one more unnecessary device between you and those tender greens. Under no circumstance do I recommend the spin cycle of the washing machine.

In any case, the ultimate goal is a salad bowl of greens that have not been overhandled or abused, dry enough so that the dressing is not diluted by water. Don't rely on the salt in the salad dressing to salt the greens. In cooking, every vegetable needs salt to draw out the juices and flavor; in the salad bowl, adding a bit of salt does the same thing for greens.

Mustard Rabbit in the Oven

Rabbit in mustard sauce is an old French dish, and there are as many versions as there are housewives. Baking it gives the rabbit a nice roasty flavor and golden color, with just a little sauce. One rabbit will feed 4 people in the context of a three-course meal, but it's no problem to do a third rabbit for larger portions, or more servings, or to have some to eat cold for lunch.

For some reason, the French mustard exported to the United States is not as pungent as the same brands bought there. So stock up on mustard when you're in France, or add a little dry mustard powder to punch up Dijon mustard here.

2 rabbits, about 2½ pounds each
Salt and pepper
¼ cup strong Dijon mustard
2 teaspoons mustard seeds, crushed
   (optional)
1½ cups Crème Fraîche (recipe
   follows) or 1¾ cups heavy cream
8 garlic cloves, sliced

½ pound thick-sliced bacon or
   pancetta, cut crosswise into
   ¼-inch-wide lardons
4 bay leaves
Thyme branches
Sage branches
A little dry white wine or chicken
   broth if needed

Ask your butcher to cut the rabbit into 6 pieces (or do it yourself with a small cleaver) as follows: Cut the saddle into 2 pieces. Divide the hind legs. Cut the foresection in half through the backbone, leaving the forelegs attached to the ribs.

Season the rabbit pieces generously with salt and freshly ground pepper and put them in a large bowl. Add the mustard, mustard seeds, crème fraîche, garlic, bacon, and bay leaves. Strip the leaves from the thyme and sage branches, chop them roughly (you'll want about 2 tablespoons of each), and add to the bowl. With your hands, smear the ingredients all over the rabbit pieces to coat evenly. Cover and let the flavors meld for an hour or two, or overnight, in the fridge.

Bring the rabbit to room temperature, and preheat the oven to 400°F. Place the rabbit pieces, along with every drop of their juicy seasoning, in two shallow, oval earthenware baking dishes just large enough to hold them.

Bake on the middle oven shelf for about 1 hour, turning the pieces as they brown. (You may remove the saddle pieces a little earlier, though, if they seem done, to keep them from overcooking. Then return at the last minute to heat through.) The rabbit should be nicely browned and the juices quite reduced. If it seems to be browning too rapidly, lay a piece of foil on top, then uncover for the last 10 minutes of cooking. If the sauce seems too reduced, splash a little white wine or chicken broth into the bottom of the baking dish, and cook for a few minutes longer.

Bring the serving vessel to the table and serve each person according to their preference: foreleg, saddle, or hindquarter. Spoon a little sauce over each serving. Accompany with the roasted parsnips. *serves 8*

crème fraîche

I have tried many commercial crème fraîche products, and some are fine, but when you make it yourself, it's cheaper and tastes better. It's easy, and you can control the quality of the ingredients. Homemade crème fraîche will not curdle when added to a sauce—not true of some commercial crème fraîche. It can be whipped like heavy cream for fruit desserts, sweetened or not. A big spoonful will enrich vegetable soups or cold salads like Celery Root Rémoulade (page 273).

Heat 2 cups organic heavy cream, not ultrapasteurized, to just under a boil. Cool to room temperature. Stir in ¼ cup plain yogurt or buttermilk. Transfer to a glass, ceramic, or stainless steel bowl and cover with a clean towel. Leave at room temperature for about 12 hours, until slightly thickened. For a tarter flavor, let it stand for 24 hours. Cover well and store, refrigerated, for up to 2 weeks.

{OTHER WAYS TO COOK A RABBIT}

RABBIT BRAISED WITH HERBS AND OLIVE OIL

Here is an easy and delicious way to cook a rabbit for a casual, bone-nibbling dinner that approximates the best pan-roasted Italian style rabbit. (In fact, it can be prepared on the stovetop with good results, but this oven version is easier.)

Chop the rabbit into 10 pieces of equal size with a cleaver, cutting right through the bones. Season the pieces well with salt and pepper, then drizzle with ½ cup olive oil and some chopped rosemary, thyme, and sage.

Place the rabbit in a shallow earthenware casserole and roast, uncovered, in a fast oven (400°F) for an hour or so, turning the pieces occasionally so they brown evenly. When the rabbit is well browned and tender, add some chopped garlic, a handful of unpitted olives, black or green, some lemon zest, and a fistful of chopped parsley. Stir and return to the oven for 5 minutes.

Serve with new potatoes, lemon wedges, and a green salad.

RABBIT ROASTED LIKE A GREEK GOAT

Split the rabbit lengthwise, and season with salt and a mixture of ground coriander seeds, allspice, bay, clove, black pepper, fennel seeds, and cinnamon. Put the halved rabbit in a baking dish, and add 3 chopped ripe tomatoes, a chopped onion, garlic, some thyme, marjoram, and rosemary, ½ cup olive oil, and ½ cup dry white wine.

Bake uncovered at 350°F for an hour and a half, more or less, turning the rabbit over in the juices occasionally. Serve with roasted potatoes and cucumbers dressed with yogurt and mint.

Parsnips have become an heirloom oddity, remembered only by an older generation. I first tasted parsnips cooked for me by a real salt-of-the-earth sixty-something big-boned American farmwife. Beryl Loobie—she was a dead ringer for Marjorie Maine, and had all that pioneer bullheadedness, but she didn't sing—was a natural cook who favored cotton housedresses, bib aprons, and lace-up boots.

I was often a guest at her table when, as a young vagabond wandering through the then-quite-hippie Pacific Northwest, my greatest ambition was to be a goatherd. Beryl and her husband, Art, raised prizewinning goats and a few other critters on a tiny rural homestead, of a kind you don't see much anymore. A few outbuildings, a small garden, the goat pens, and a two-room cottage were the extent of their possessions. To me it seemed idyllic.

That day, Beryl yanked those parsnips from the vegetable patch on the way back from chores, then washed, peeled, and roasted them in a cast-iron pan. "You might as well stay for dinner," she told me. "I've got some chicken backs." Then she went on to produce a frugal but delicious meal of gravy from scratch, instant mashed potatoes, homemade white bread, homemade pickles, and homemade pie. She managed this despite the inconvenience of a broken arm (the result of wrestling hay bales in the goat barn). Of the roasted chicken backs, crisp and well seasoned, barely meaty, she said, "I just wanted you to think you were having chicken." When I praised the parsnips, she said, "Well, it's just parsnips." But they were so crisp, brown, tender, and sweet, I thought they were the best thing I'd ever eaten.

Beryl raised three boys, sometimes with the help of a harness to keep them from straying ("Never hurt 'em any!"), and somehow found time to teach a cake-decorating class at a nearby church. To see her, you'd never guess she had a soft side. But for everyone's birthday, she would set out her bright-colored Crisco-based frostings and fashion a cake adorned with sugary miniature daffodils, jonquils, and roses. She was especially good with daffodils.

Parsnips Epiphany-Style

This old-fashioned, nearly forgotten root vegetable is lovely roasted and slightly caramelized. Parsnips look like pale carrots, but their flavor is a heady cross between butternut squash and chestnuts.

4 to 5 pounds parsnips   3 tablespoons olive oil
Salt and pepper

Preheat the oven to 375°F. Peel the parsnips and quarter them lengthwise. With a paring knife, remove the central core (in my experience, even small parsnips have a hard core). If the parsnips are smallish, just trim the ends; if larger, cut them into 3-inch lengths.

Season well with salt and pepper and toss with the olive oil, then install the parsnips in an earthenware dish or roasting pan. Bake for 45 minutes or so, until they are fork-tender and lightly browned. They can be cooked in advance and reheated.

Apple Tart

This is the plainest—and best—apple tart. It is good at room temperature, better if slightly warm. If possible, bake the tart during dinner, then let it cool a bit before serving.

My friend Ernestine, raised in rural Idaho, had a recipe for what she called Mormon pie dough. She used it for fruit pies and for a memorable sauerkraut and pork sausage pie. The original recipe begins, "First stir up an egg . . . ," and it calls for using all lard. For desserts, I prefer to use all butter; for a savory pie, I use lard. Either way, the pastry has wonderful flakiness and is easy to handle.

2 cups all-purpose flour,
   plus extra for sprinkling
½ pound (2 sticks) cold butter,
   in thin slices
½ teaspoon salt
1 egg, beaten, plus enough
   ice water to make ½ cup

8 medium crisp apples,
   about 3 pounds
1 cup sugar for the glaze,
   plus extra for sprinkling
   on the apples
1 cup water

Put the flour, butter, and salt in a bowl. With your fingers, work the butter into the flour until it looks mealy, with some large flecks of butter remaining. Pour the egg–ice water mixture into the bowl and quickly knead the dough for only a minute or two, until it comes together. It will be soft, a little sticky, and, though gathered together, a little rough looking.

Sprinkle the dough with a little flour and pat into a rectangle about 1 inch thick. Wrap and refrigerate for at least an hour, or overnight.

Divide the pastry in half (there will be enough for 2 tarts; you can freeze one half for later). Roll out the pastry to a rectangle, approximately 11 by 16 inches, using a 15½-by-10½-inch baking sheet as a template.

Transfer the dough to the baking sheet and let it relax, then trim the edges to fit the pan with a little going slightly up the sides. Cover with plastic wrap and refrigerate.

Peel the apples and cut into quarters. Remove the cores and use to make a glaze as follows: Combine the 1 cup sugar and 1 cup water with the cores. Stir at first to dissolve sugar, then simmer to a thick syrup. Strain and reserve. (Or use honey or good apricot jam, thinned, for a glaze.) Slice the apples as thin as possible. Arrange the apple slices over the pastry in 5 rows, overlapping them like cards in solitaire. At this point the tart can be covered with plastic wrap and refrigerated for up to 8 hours. (It's okay if the apples darken.)

Preheat the oven to 375°F. Sprinkle the sugar generously over the apples and bake until they are beautifully browned and the pastry is crisp, about 45 minutes. Cool on a rack.

Just before serving, reheat the glaze. Slide the tart from the pan onto a cutting board. Paint the apples with the warmed glaze. Slice into small rectangles to serve.

a cold spring

Oysters on the Half-Shell

Chicory Salad with Lemon and Anchovy

Lobster Risotto

Ambrosia

We called it stormy Monday—a cold March day on the tail end of a New York winter. A group of friends had planned a night on the town, but given the nasty weather—the forecast was for more severe storms—we decided it would clearly be more fun to stay in. Eating well would be our revenge once again.

The plan was to get a fire going in the fireplace at my sister's, chill a lot of Champagne, and take our time cooking dinner. We had no menu in mind, preferring to head for the market and employ the "take a look, see what shines" approach. The Union Square Greenmarket had lots of Italian chicories: radicchio, Treviso, speckled escarole, pale blanched curly endive, rose-hued Belgian endive, and dandelion (not a true chicory, but similarly bitter-sweet). A sparkling salad took shape before our eyes. Unmoved by the butcher shop (meat did not raise our spirits that day), we pressed on to the fish store, where we discovered fat oysters glistening with promise, somehow enhancing the wetness of the weather. The group was still growing, so panfrying fish wouldn't work. We needed something

elastic, like a stew or a roast. When I got to the lobster tank it was suddenly clear: lobster risotto.

Comforting and elegant, simple and fancy at the same time. And you just can't get a good risotto in a restaurant. You have to wait for risotto; risotto doesn't wait for you. Perfect. Since we didn't yet know how many people were coming for dinner, I'd get a final count and, if necessary, add little more rice to the pot. I secretly hoped there would be leftovers so I could make risotto fritters the next day for lunch.

Oysters on the Half-Shell

Get someone to teach you how to open an oyster. It's really not difficult, and it really *is* all in the wrist. My trick is to keep a few oyster knives around and give a demonstration: soon everyone wants to open oysters.

I like oysters just plain, or maybe with a wedge of lemon. Forget about sauces like mignonette or "cocktail" sauce. All oysters really need is a glass of Champagne or Sancerre.

Ask a good fishmonger to get you a box of five dozen oysters for the day you'll serve them. Keep them cold in an ice chest or even outside, if it's not freezing. Wash the oysters briefly under cold running water to remove mud and bits of shell. Put them in a basket or pile them up on crushed ice.

Set up a little oyster station on a kitchen counter near the sink, with a small cutting board, a few kitchen towels, some oyster knives, and a receptacle for the shells. Enlist an assistant or two.

Open 12 oysters at a time, discarding the top shells, and making sure to sever the oysters from the bottom shells. Line a small platter with evergreens, fresh seaweed, or rock salt to keep the oysters from tipping over and spilling their liquor. Pass the platter for immediate stand-up slurping.

Chicory Salad with Lemon and Anchovy

A chicory salad is a gorgeous mixture of colors—deep reds, pinks, and pale green-yellows. Here its agreeable bittersweet flavor is mellowed by a lemony vinaigrette, spiked with a good touch of anchovy.

This salad would make a great first course for another meal with the addition of Soft-Center Hard-Cooked Eggs (page 154), garlic toast (see page 182), and Parmigiano shavings. The dressing works well with romaine-type lettuces too, and with boiled leeks and potatoes.

6 anchovy fillets

½ cup milk

4 garlic cloves

Salt and pepper

Finely chopped zest and
   juice of 1 lemon

Champagne vinegar

1 tablespoon Dijon mustard

¾ cup olive oil

8 large handfuls assorted chicories—
   use a combination of radicchio,
   Treviso, escarole, curly endive,
   Belgian endive, and dandelion—
   washed, dried, and torn into
   large pieces

Rinse the anchovy fillets in a bowl of warm water, then soak in the milk for 15 minutes to mellow (see page 172). Remove the anchovies from the milk and blot on paper towels.

Mash the garlic with the anchovies in a mortar. Add a little salt to help create a paste. Add a little finely chopped lemon zest, the juice of half the lemon, and a splash of champagne vinegar. Stir in the mustard, and, gradually, the olive oil, until you have a thickish vinaigrette. Check the seasoning, and correct with lemon juice, salt, and/or freshly ground black pepper. The vinaigrette should be zesty but not too acid.

In a large wide salad bowl, toss the chicories with a little salt. Dress the leaves lightly at first, tossing well with your hands to coat well. Taste a leaf and add a little more dressing as necessary. The salad tastes best about 5 minutes after it's dressed.

Lobster Risotto

It may seem counterintuitive, but risotto's particular nature—it requires constant surveillance—makes it perfect for a big dinner.

2 large onions, finely diced

8 tablespoons (1 stick) butter

Salt and pepper

¼ cup olive oil

2 cups Carnaroli or Arborio rice

½ teaspoon saffron, crumbled

1 bay leaf

2 garlic cloves, finely chopped

6 cups warm Lobster Broth
    (recipe follows) or chicken broth

3½ cups cooked lobster meat,
    roughly chopped
      (from 4 or 5 live lobsters)

3 tablespoons chopped parsley

2 teaspoons chopped thyme

2 tablespoons finely cut chives

1 teaspoon grated lemon zest

Spicy Lobster Mayonnaise
    (recipe follows)

In a heavy-bottomed pot (enameled cast iron works well), sauté the onions in the butter, adding a little salt, until they are translucent, 5 minutes or so. Increase the heat and add the olive oil, rice, saffron, bay leaf, garlic, and a little more salt. Stir until the rice is sizzling and aromatic. Add 2 cups broth and bring to a boil (from this point, it will take 15 to 20 minutes to cook the rice).

Set the fire to keep the liquid at a brisk simmer. This is critical. If the flame is too low, the rice will become soggy; if is too high, the liquid will simply evaporate instead of being absorbed by the rice. You'll need to keep adjusting the heat to keep the risotto simmering correctly. Stirring occasionally, allow the broth to reduce almost completely, until little sinkholes appear on the surface. Add another cup of broth and repeat. Adjust the seasoning with each addition of liquid. Add a final cup of broth and repeat. A little more salt, or more broth, may be required. When the rice is done, it should be just al dente and a bit soupy.

Just before serving, add the cooked lobster meat and season it with salt and pepper. Sprinkle the herbs and lemon zest over the lobster, then gently mix with a wooden spoon—avoid smashing the rice. Add a little more warm broth, so the risotto is easily spoonable. Serve the risotto in warmed shallow soup plates, and pass a bowl of the spicy lobster mayonnaise, so each person can add a small spoonful.

serves 8–10

lobster broth

Bring 2 gallons heavily salted water to a rolling boil. Add 5 live 1-pound lobsters and boil for 12 minutes. Remove and let cool. Remove the meat from the lobsters, reserving the shells. Eat the knuckles for a cook's treat. Coarsely chop the tail and claw meat (this should yield about 3½ cups meat) and keep at cool room temperature.

Put the lobster shells in a small stockpot. Add a few cloves of garlic and chopped carrot, leek, and onion. Cover with 4 quarts water and simmer for 20 to 30 minutes. Strain the broth. Reserve 6 cups for the risotto.

Boil down the remaining broth to make a dark concentrated lobster reduction, if you wish, or freeze the rest for another day.

spicy lobster mayonnaise

A dab of spicy mayonnaise is the sauce for the risotto. I believe it's important to make your own mayonnaise. It is not hard to do, and no matter how many cookbooks or food magazines recommend mayonnaise from a jar as a good substitute, I strongly, vehemently disagree.

Whisk 2 egg yolks in a bowl. Slowly stir in olive oil, a spoonful at a time, until an emulsion forms. As the sauce thickens, continue whisking and adding oil in a slow, steady stream.

When the mayonnaise is quite thick (you'll have used about a cup of oil at this point), thin with a teaspoon of reduced lobster broth or water. Season with salt, pepper, and a good pinch of ground red pepper, such as piment d'Espelette or hot paprika. Whisk in another ½ cup olive oil. Thin again, and adjust the seasoning. Add a few drops of lemon juice or red wine vinegar, and a little more reduction or water. The finished mayonnaise should be the texture of softly whipped cream.

{VARIATION} PLAIN HOMEMADE MAYONNAISE

Replace lobster reduction with a few drops of lemon juice. Omit the red pepper. Use half olive and half peanut oil for a milder-tasting mayonnaise.

{FROM LEFTOVERS} RISOTTO CAKES

If you have risotto left, form it into small cakes, patting them with your hands as if making oval hamburgers.

Dip the cakes in flour seasoned with salt and pepper, then dip in beaten egg. Coat the cakes in bread crumbs and fry them in an inch of olive oil until golden, about 4 minutes per side. Serve with a dab of the Spicy Lobster Mayonnaise and a green salad.

Ambrosia

My mother's cousin Jeannie was raised in the South, and she was probably responsible for making ambrosia a "company" dessert in our family, always served in cut-glass goblets. When I ask friends if they know about ambrosia, they say, "You mean the one with the miniature marshmallows?" "No," I reply, "the one with the canned pineapple and shredded coconut."

4 pink grapefruits

6 navel oranges

8 blood oranges

One 6-ounce can crushed pineapple or
    a cup or so of fresh pineapple

8 kumquats

Sugar if necessary

1 cup organic coconut flakes
    (sweetened or not)

With a sharp serrated knife, cut off the top and bottom of the grapefruits, navel oranges, and blood oranges, then peel, making sure to remove the white pith. Working over a bowl, section the grapefruits into wedges, cutting between the membranes. Before discarding the grapefruit carcasses, squeeze them over the wedges—they will yield a cup or two of juice. Slice the navel oranges and blood oranges crosswise into ¼-inch disks and add them to the bowl. I add the crushed pineapple mostly for nostalgia's sake. If you wish, use chunks of sweet fresh pineapple.

Slice the kumquats into the thinnest rounds possible, then mix them gently with the other citrus, to avoid breaking the fruit. Taste the juice, adding sugar only if it seems too tart. Transfer the compote to a serving bowl, cover, and refrigerate for up to several hours.

Just before serving, sprinkle the coconut over. Sweetened flaked coconut is traditional, but it's nice to use unsweetened too.

supper of the lamb

Warm Asparagus Vinaigrette

Shoulder of Spring Lamb with Flageolet Beans and Olive Relish

Rum Baba with Cardamom

Ask any cook who has worked with me—they'll tell you I'm a fanatic about asparagus. I've driven kitchen apprentices half crazy making them go through entire cases to choose only the most perfect spears. I adore asparagus, but it must be freshly picked or I'm not interested. I wouldn't even think about eating asparagus shipped from Chile or Peru in November. I scoff at the early asparagus that arrives around Valentine's Day. I'll just wait for the real thing, thank you. It means spring has arrived, and it's worth the wait.

When asparagus time does roll around, everyone in the market has it. But all asparagus is not equal. Asparagus must be ultrafresh; it really does not keep. Older asparagus tastes grassy and dull; newly harvested asparagus is sweet and toothsome. Oddly, asparagus continues to grow after it's picked. The stalks keep pushing upward, attempting to fulfill their natural inclination: going to seed. As the asparagus grows, the meaty sweetness vanishes, the spears get stringy looking, and the tops open up. Don't buy those.

Look for stalks that are firm, shiny, and unblemished, with tightly closed tips. Check the bottoms to make sure they're freshly cut. And you need to snap the

tough ends off. And while you may have heard that those ends are good in soup, I can assure you that it is not a good idea. They're far too woody.

Okay. About peeling. I peel the stalks only if they're fat. It's a texture thing. The skin on fat asparagus spears doesn't ever soften. Peel them so that you're biting into the sweet flesh instead of tough skin.

Warm Asparagus Vinaigrette

4 to 5 pounds fresh green asparagus

2 small shallots, finely diced

2 to 3 tablespoons red wine vinegar

Salt and pepper

¾ cup olive oil

Break off the tough ends of the asparagus spears and discard. If the spears are quite thick, peel them with a sharp vegetable peeler. Fill two large pots with 4 quarts water each, salt the water heavily, and bring to a rolling boil.

While the water comes to a boil, make the vinaigrette: In a small bowl, macerate the shallots in 2 tablespoons red wine vinegar with a little salt for a few minutes. Then whisk in the olive oil and a little freshly ground pepper. Taste and reseason the vinaigrette, adding a little more vinegar and salt if necessary—but don't make it too tart.

Just before you're ready to eat, put the asparagus spears in the boiling water and let them simmer briskly for 3 to 8 minutes, depending on their size. Remove them when they are firmly al dente and still bright green (the best way to check is to retrieve one spear and taste it). Lift the asparagus spears from the water with a large strainer—a wide Asian bamboo-handled wire spider works well—and let them drain on a clean kitchen towel for a couple of minutes. As they sit, they will continue to cook a little bit.

Pile the spears onto a platter. Sprinkle lightly with salt and freshly ground pepper. Whisk the vinaigrette and spoon it over the asparagus.

Shoulder of Spring Lamb with Flageolet Beans and Olive Relish

True spring lamb is not easily found here, as most American lamb (sourced from New Zealand) is raised to a larger size. But some good butchers carry or can order it, and a few excellent American farms now specialize in young pastured lamb. Otherwise, ask your butcher for the smallest lamb shoulder roasts possible. Tender young spring lamb is best cooked almost medium, with a crisp roasty exterior. I'm crazy about pale green flageolet beans, a classic lamb accompaniment. Their wonderful nutty flavor pairs well, too, with olive oil and thyme.

1½ pounds dried flageolet beans
   (about 3 cups)
1 large onion, quartered
1 bay leaf
A few unpeeled garlic cloves,
   plus 4 garlic cloves sliced
Thyme sprigs
Salt and pepper

2 boneless spring lamb shoulders,
   about 3 pounds each, tied into roasts
Rosemary sprigs
Fruity olive oil
2 cups dry white wine,
   such as Sauvignon Blanc
1 small bunch flat-leaf parsley
Olive Relish (recipe follows)

Pick over the flageolet beans and rinse them well. Set them to boil in a large heavy pot with enough cold water to cover by 3 inches. Add the onion, bay leaf, unpeeled garlic, and a large thyme sprig. When the water boils, turn the flame to low and let the beans simmer gently until quite tender, about 1 hour if they are from a recent crop, longer if not.

Once the beans are done, stir a good spoonful of salt into the cooking liquid, and let the beans cool in their broth. The beans can be cooked early in the day, or even a day ahead and refrigerated.

Preheat the oven to 375°F . Season the lamb roasts with salt and pepper. Insert the slices of garlic in the loose flesh on the underside of the roasts. Lay a few rosemary and thyme sprigs in the bottom of a roasting pan. Set the lamb on top.

Drizzle a little olive oil over the lamb. Pour the white wine into the pan.

Roast the lamb for 45 minutes to an hour, or until the exterior is nicely browned and the internal temperature reads 130°F. Remove the lamb to a platter, cover loosely, and let it rest.

Scrape up the juices from the bottom of the roasting pan with a wooden spoon, taking care to dissolve the caramelized brown bits clinging here and there. Pour the pan juices through a fine-meshed strainer into a small saucepan. Skim off any surface fat, and reheat the pan juices just before serving.

Drain the flageolets, reserving their liquid, and put them in a shallow pan. Season them with salt and pepper, a little chopped thyme, and a good splash of fruity olive oil. Add a cup of the bean broth and reheat the beans gently.

Chop the parsley and slice the lamb.

Pour the flageolets onto a warmed platter and arrange the lamb slices over the beans. Spoon some of the warm pan juices over the lamb. Scatter the parsley over everything and serve. Pass the olive relish, thinned with pan juices if you like.

serves 8–10

olive relish

A wonderful condiment to have on hand, perfect with the roast lamb, this relish can also enhance grilled fish or roast chicken, or liven up a sandwich or a pizza. Well covered, it will keep for a week in the refrigerator.

1 cup oil-cured Moroccan olives,
   pitted

1 cup Niçoise olives, pitted

2 teaspoons capers, well rinsed

2 small garlic cloves, smashed to a
   paste with a little salt

Finely chopped zest of
   half a small lemon

Juice of 1 small lemon

1 teaspoon chopped thyme

2 anchovy fillets, well rinsed and
   chopped (optional)

About ¾ cup olive oil

Salt and pepper

Pinch of cayenne or red pepper flakes
   (optional)

Put the olives, capers, garlic, lemon zest, lemon juice, thyme, anchovies, if using, and ½ cup olive oil in a blender or food processor and grind to a paste. Make the texture of the relish to your preference—rough or smooth. Pulsing the ingredients makes it rough; for a smoother texture, let the machine run for a few minutes. (For a more rustic version, hand-chop the ingredients.)

Scrape the olive relish into a small bowl. Taste and adjust the seasoning, adding pepper—or a little cayenne or red pepper flakes —as desired and salt if necessary. Thin with a little more olive oil to loosen the paste. Makes about 2 cups relish.

Rum Baba with Cardamom

Rum baba is one of those desserts people either love or hate. If you grew up with syrup-soaked cakes, you'll adore it. If not, probably not. French restaurants make a big production of their babas au rhum, hauling a cart of exotic vintage rums over to the table and letting the diner choose the rum to be poured over the baba.

In Italy, you can find a rum-soaked cake in any bar, to accompany a strong espresso for a late-morning pick-me-up. The Italians and the French are still arguing about who taught what to whom when.

You can make a big baba, but I like small individual ones. A little whipped cream is good alongside, or vanilla or cardamom-flavored ice cream. Babas are also good with fresh orange sections, strawberries, or sliced mango.

The babas and the syrup can be made a day ahead, then assembled for serving. To restore the fresh-baked taste, crisp the babas in a medium oven for 15 minutes, then cool before soaking them in the rum syrup.

2 teaspoons active dry yeast

¼ cup warm water

2 tablespoons sugar

4 large eggs

¼ teaspoon salt

2 cups all-purpose flour, or as needed

8 tablespoons (1 stick) sweet butter,
   softened

Rum Syrup (recipe follows)

Barely Whipped Cream
   (recipe follows)

Dissolve the yeast in the warm water in a small bowl. Stir in the sugar and leave the mixture at room temperature for 5 to 10 minutes, until it becomes active and bubbly.

Beat the eggs with the salt in a small bowl, then add the yeast mixture. In a large mixing bowl (or in the bowl of a standing mixer), combine the flour and butter. Mash the butter (with your hands or the paddle attachment) into the flour until it is well absorbed. Add the egg mixture and mix well with a wooden spoon (or the machine) for about 5 minutes, until the dough comes together (at this stage, the dough is too soft to mix by hand).

When you have a nice soft but somewhat sticky dough, cover the bowl and put it in a warm sunny room or its makeshift equivalent for an hour or so, until risen to nearly double in size. Push down the dough, cover with plastic wrap, and refrigerate for several hours or overnight.

Turn the dough out onto a floured surface and knead lightly to form a soft smooth log. Cut the log into 12 pieces of equal size, then roll each piece into a little ball. Put the little balls into buttered baba molds, muffin tins, or small ramekins. Place them on a baking sheet, cover lightly with plastic wrap, and put them in a warm spot for 30 to 40 minutes, until they puff to twice their size.

Preheat the oven to 400°F. Bake the babas for 15 minutes, or until they firm up and their tops are brown. Invert the babas onto the baking sheet (their bottoms will be pale) and return them to the oven to brown and crisp for another 5 minutes. Cool the babas on a rack.

Two hours before serving, put the babas in a deep baking dish, top side down. Pour the syrup over the babas, and let them soak for 5 minutes. Turn them bottom side down and let them soak again. Now put the babas in a deep serving platter, reserving the syrup, cover, and refrigerate until serving time.

To serve, garnish the babas with some of the orange peel, lemon zest, cardamom, and kumquat from the syrup. Pour a few tablespoons of syrup over each baba, and pass the remaining syrup, the rum bottle, and the bowl of whipped cream. Eat the babas with soupspoons.

rum syrup

I prefer dark rum for this syrup. The syrup can be made a few hours in advance, or up to a day ahead.

½ cup honey

¾ cup sugar

1 cup water

1 cinnamon stick

A few cloves

12 green cardamom pods

Strips of orange and lemon zest

A few kumquats, sliced (optional)

½ cup rum, or more to taste

In a saucepan, stir together all ingredients except the rum until the sugar dissolves. Bring to a boil, then lower the heat and simmer for 10 minutes. Add the rum, and cool to room temperature.

barely whipped cream

Put a cup of organic—not ultrapasturized—cream in a bowl. Add a tablespoon of sugar. Beat with a wire whisk or an old-fashioned egg beater (a handheld mixer can turn the cream too stiff very fast) until the cream has a light, billowy consistency; if you beat the cream until it just falls from a spoon, it'll taste lighter and feel more voluptuous. Stop beating *before* peaks form. I like to pass the bowl around so friends can take a turn.

salmon on my mind

Fried Egg Soup

Wild Salmon with Vietnamese Cucumbers

Rose-Scented Strawberries

In the kitchen at Chez Panisse, even though we have always served one set menu nightly, designed for seasonality and balance—and now even an alternative vegetarian menu—we still get an amazing number of requests for changes. We always accommodate requests based on allergies or dietary requirements, but increasingly the requests we're hearing are rooted in a fear of food.

Our servings of meat are restrained, just a few slices. We always leave the fat on the duck breast and the fat on the pork—it tastes good, and you need some fat in your diet. Yet more and more diners are leaving the fat on the plate. It's kind of astonishing, because the style of food at Chez Panisse emulates the best of home cooking: light-handed, vegetable-heavy. We use hardly any butter or cream, and desserts are usually based on fruit. If it's a splurge, it's a healthy splurge.

For me, balanced eating means a lot of vegetables with a little meat, not a lot of meat with few vegetables. But it doesn't preclude fats or oil or butter or saucisson or even foie gras, in judicious quantities. My idea of balanced eating goes beyond the balanced meal to the balanced week, the balanced year.

Still, as the seasons change, you anticipate a shift in the kind of cooking you'll be doing. After the heavier, browner food of winter—the wild mushrooms, the red wine braises—spring's arrival means a different kind of craving. You want green. Not just for its tonic effect, but also for the bright, fresh flavors you've been missing. Light soups, tangy herbs, sweet peas. And fish. For me, spring fish means wild salmon. Its arrival is a joy, its flavor a welcome astonishment.

Fried Egg Soup

A runny egg in a bowl of garlicky chicken broth is a pleasurable way to begin a meal. The quality and freshness of the egg matters most. Poached eggs are good, but for this soup I like to fry the eggs for more flavor. Green garlic shoots come to market in early spring. Like tiny leeks or green onions, they need their outer layer removed, and then they can be slivered, chopped, or pounded to add to a dish. The perfume of green garlic shows best with minimal cooking.

8 organic eggs
Olive oil
Salt and pepper
12 cups Light Chicken Stock
   (recipe follows)
2 bunches green garlic shoots, thinly
   sliced (or substitute 4 garlic cloves,
   thinly sliced)

One 1-inch piece of ginger, peeled and
   finely chopped
3 cups spinach or bok choy leaves,
   in thin ribbons
4 scallions, slivered

Fry the eggs sunny-side up in a little olive oil, seasoning them well with salt and pepper and leaving them rather runny. The eggs can be fried up to an hour ahead and held on a baking sheet at room temperature.

In a large pot, bring the chicken stock to a simmer. Add the garlic and simmer for 5 minutes. Add the ginger and cook for a few minutes more. Taste and add salt as needed.

Just before serving, add the spinach or bok choy to the hot soup. It will just take a minute to wilt.

For each serving, put a fried egg in a warmed shallow soup plate. Ladle over the hot broth and sprinkle with the scallions. Serve the soup immediately.

light chicken stock

It is so easy to boil up a little chicken stock, and the result is always so much better than what you can buy. Beware the canned or cubed—they never taste real. And I am bewildered by those shelf-stable stocks that come in boxes (some labeled organic!). Their flavor, color, and consistency seem odd.

For a quick chicken stock, start with 4 pounds meaty chicken wings in 4 quarts water. Add a finely slivered leek, a chopped onion and carrot, a thyme branch, and a few peppercorns. Simmer for 40 minutes, then strain and skim. This makes a light, tasty chicken stock you can use immediately.

{OTHER EGG SOUPS}

PROVENÇAL EGG SOUP

Omit the ginger. Simmer a few sage leaves in the broth with the garlic. Float the fried eggs on rounds of toasted baguette.

MEXICAN EGG SOUP

Omit the ginger. Garnish with sliced serrano chiles, a handful of cilantro leaves, fried tortilla strips, and a generous squeeze of lime.

Wild Salmon with Vietnamese Cucumbers

Wild salmon is the healthiest and most sustainable salmon, and it's also the best tasting by far. Farmed salmon are as bland and flavorless as factory chicken. They're fed a dubious diet and require antibiotics to control the disease that inevitably results from their crowded, polluting pens. When they escape, farmed fish endanger native species. Need any more reasons to go wild? "Fish gotta swim" for both flavor and health.

To accompany the salmon and cucumbers, serve plain steamed jasmine rice and sweet potatoes roasted in the skin.

A side of wild salmon, about 4 pounds   Mint, cilantro, and basil sprigs
Salt and pepper   Lime wedges
Olive oil   Vietnamese cucumbers (recipe follows)

Bring the salmon to room temperature, and preheat the oven to 350°F. Put the fish on a baking sheet, and season with salt and pepper. Drizzle a little olive oil over the salmon and rub it into the flesh.

Bake for 20 to 25 minutes, just until juices appear on the surface. When probed with a fork at the thickest part, the salmon should be moist—cooked through, but barely. Transfer the fish to a warmed platter, and let it rest at least 5 minutes before serving.

Before bringing the fish to the table, embellish the platter with mint, cilantro, and basil sprigs, and surround the salmon with lime wedges. At the table, break the salmon into rough portions. Pass the cucumbers to be spooned over the fish.

vietnamese cucumbers

This easy salad is more like a relish and can be made according to your own taste: very spicy, which is how I like it, or quite restrained. Its virtue is that it can refresh almost any dish. Look for palm sugar in Asian or Indian markets, or substitute Mexican piloncillo or raw brown sugar.

4 large cucumbers

Salt and pepper

Vietnamese fish sauce (*nuoc mam*) or
    Thai fish sauce (*nam pla*)

A 1-inch piece of ginger, peeled and cut
    into fine julienne

Palm sugar

Serranos or jalapeños or
    fresh Thai chiles

2 or 3 limes

Mint sprigs

Basil sprigs

Thinly sliced scallions or sweet onion

Peel the cucumbers, cut them lengthwise in half, and remove the seeds with a spoon if they are large. Slice the cucumbers into thickish half-moons and put them in a large bowl. Season with salt and pepper, sprinkle lightly with fish sauce, then add the ginger and a couple of tablespoons of palm sugar. Toss well, and let the cucumbers sit for 5 minutes or so.

Add a good spoonful of finely chopped serrano or jalapeño chiles (seeds removed, if desired, to lessen spiciness) or finely slivered Thai chiles. Squeeze over the juice of 2 limes and toss again, then cover and refrigerate till serving.

Just before serving add a fistful of roughly chopped mint and basil leaves. Taste and adjust the seasoning with lime juice as well as salt and pepper. Garnish with thinly sliced scallions or paper-thin slices of sweet onion.　　　*serves 8–10*

{VARIATION} HERBED CUCUMBERS

This salad is not spicy but it is refreshing. Peel the cucumbers, thickly slice them, and season with salt, pepper, and lemon juice. Chill them in a serving bowl for at least 20 minutes.

Just before serving, finely mince a mixture of the following herbs: parsley, chervil, dill, basil, tarragon, mint, and chives. Scatter over the cucumbers, toss briefly, and serve immediately.

Rose-Scented Strawberries

Strawberries are botanically related to roses, and they taste wonderful together. Try to find locally grown organic strawberries. It is better to wait for good strawberries to come into season than to give in to mass-produced, chemically fertilized, and pesticide-laden fruit (nonorganic strawberries are the most heavily dosed fruit). Rose syrup, too, can be artificially tricked up. Look for a brand made with only roses and sugar. Serve with Barely Whipped Cream (page 69), if you like.

4 pints organic strawberries	Kirsch
Sugar	Organic rose syrup

Rinse the berries briefly with cold water and lay them on a kitchen towel. Discard any imperfect fruit (or make jam with it).

With a paring knife or huller, remove the leaves and cores, taking care to leave the natural berry shape. Cut larger berries into wedges or slices. Cover and keep at room temperature until ready to serve.

Just before serving, put the strawberries in a mixing bowl, sprinkle lightly with sugar, and splash with a little kirsch. Add 2 teaspoons rose syrup and toss gently until all is glistening. Put the berries in a beautiful bowl and take them to the table.

duck for dinner

Crabmeat and Parsley Salad

Five-Spice Duck with Buttered Turnips and Fried Ginger

Rhubarb Kumquat Compote

You are probably not surprised to learn that I am not a fan of fusion. They can keep their wasabi aïoli, thank you very much. But though my training and inclination usually push me in a European—or at least a Mediterranean—direction, there's a dim sum–eating, noodle-soup–slurping part of me too.

In both cities where I live—San Francisco and Paris—robust Asian communities have seductive markets offering such enticing ingredients it's impossible for a curious cook to remain stubbornly, foolishly Western. I've found ways to enhance much of my cooking with the subtle use of ginger and sesame. I think Chinese five-spice powder is a genius seasoning. Its classic combination of pepper, star anise, clove, fennel seed, and cinnamon can perfectly perfume duck, pork, or any other meat.

Recently I was at the market, prowling for dinner as usual. I thought I wanted to make a spring duck stew, had nearly decided on a ducky variation of a spring lamb navarin, and had just bought some duck legs, when I noticed little bunches of sweet young turnips with their bright green tops smiling up at me.

Duck with turnips is a traditional combination in classic French cooking. Nothing wrong with that.

But suddenly the notion of duck and turnips turned Asian on me. I am a great fan of Chinese-style roast duck, and also of those heavenly griddled turnip cakes served in dim sum parlors. So I changed gears, went with the new idea, and bought some fresh ginger. The result was a French-style braise with Chinese flavors. It might sound like fusion or new-wave cooking to you, but the result is extremely subtle, and it doesn't overpower a good bottle of red wine.

Crabmeat and Parsley Salad

Make this only when you can find perfectly fresh shelled crab at your fish store.

2 pounds crabmeat

1 bunch scallions

1 bunch flat-leaf parsley

4 heads Belgian endive

1 lemon

Salt and pepper

2 tablespoons Asian sesame oil

Pick over the crabmeat for any bits of shell and put it in a bowl. Refrigerate until just before serving.

Sliver the scallions, both the white and pale green parts. Pick the leaves from the parsley. If the leaves are small and tender, leave them whole; otherwise, sliver them. Separate and trim the leaves of the endive. Zest a teaspoon or so of the lemon.

To assemble the salad, squeeze half the juice of the lemon over the crabmeat. Add the lemon zest, scallions, and parsley and season lightly with salt and pepper. Drizzle with the sesame oil and toss very gently. Taste and adjust the seasoning with more lemon juice if necessary.

Pile the crab salad into a platter. Surround with the endive leaves. Serve immediately.

Five-Spice Duck Legs with Buttered Turnips and Fried Ginger

Five-spice powder is available in most Asian groceries, but it's easy to make your own (see below).

12 duck legs, preferably Pekin
    (Long Island)

Salt and pepper

2 teaspoons five-spice powder,
    homemade (recipe follows)
    or store-bought

2 large onions, finely diced

2 tablespoons chopped ginger

6 garlic cloves, smashed to a paste
    with a little salt

8 cups chicken broth, preferably
    Dark Chicken Stock (page 26)

2 tablespoons cornstarch

¼ cup cold water

Fried Ginger (recipe follows)

Buttered Turnips (recipe follows)

Trim the duck legs (save the trimmings to make rendered duck fat; see Note page 274). Season the duck generously with salt and pepper, sprinkle with the five-spice powder, and massage the seasoning into the meat. Refrigerate the seasoned duck legs overnight, or at least for several hours.

Preheat the oven to 400°F. Heat a dry cast-iron frying pan over medium heat, and slowly brown the duck legs (in batches or use 2 pans), skin side down. As the duck legs cook, they will give off a fair amount of fat. When the skin is nicely browned, after 10 minutes or so, remove the legs and set aside. Pour off all but ½ inch of the fat.

Add the onions to the pan and cook until golden, then add the ginger, garlic, and some salt and pepper. Cook 2 minutes more, then drain the onions in a colander, reserving the perfumed fat for another purpose (such as for frying potatoes). It will keep for 2 months in the fridge.

Put the onions in a shallow earthenware casserole. Lay the duck legs skin side up over the onions in a single layer. Put the casserole, uncovered, in the oven and let the legs roast for 10 to 15 minutes. Meanwhile, heat the chicken stock.

Add the stock to the casserole and continue cooking until the stock comes to a full simmer. Then reduce the heat to 375°F, cover, and cook for about an hour, until the duck legs are tender when probed with a paring knife.

Uncover the baking dish and keep in the oven to let the duck legs crisp for about 5 minutes. Remove the duck legs to a deep serving platter and cover loosely to keep warm.

Pour the cooking liquid into a saucepan and let stand briefly, then degrease. Taste and adjust the seasoning if necessary. Bring to a simmer. Mix the cornstarch with the cold water, add to the sauce, and simmer for 2 minutes to thicken slightly.

Pour the sauce over the duck legs. Sprinkle with the fried ginger, and serve with the buttered turnips.   *serves 12*

five-spice powder

Grind 1 tablespoon each Sichuan pepper (or black peppercorns), star anise, crushed cinnamon stick, cloves, and fennel seeds in a spice grinder. Store in a glass jar.

fried ginger

Crisp lightly fried ginger makes a lovely garnish for meat dishes or vegetables.

6 ounces ginger   Salt
2 cups peanut or vegetable oil

Peel the ginger—using the "spoon trick" (see Note)—and cut it into thin slices. A mandoline is helpful but not necessary. Cut the ginger slices crosswise into slivers. They should look like flimsy matchsticks.

Heat the peanut oil to 400° F in a small deep pot. Carefully fry the ginger a handful at a time until the slivers are barely golden, about 2 minutes. Drain on paper towels. Sprinkle the ginger lightly with salt. Leave at room temperature until needed, up to several hours.

Try this trick—scrape an inverted teaspoon lightly over fresh ginger. The thin skin comes right off, as if by magic.

buttered turnips

If you have larger turnips, peel them and cut into wedges, and cook them a little longer. Instead of turnip greens, you can use 1 pound tender mustard greens or spinach to finish the dish.

4 bunches small turnips with greens, 4 to 5 pounds	2 tablespoons butter
	Salt and pepper

Cut the greens from the turnips. Wash the greens in a basin of cold water, lift out, and set aside. Cut the turnips into halves or quarters so they are all roughly the same size. Rinse and drain.

Melt the butter in a large heavy-bottomed pot. Add the turnips and season with salt and pepper. Let the turnips simmer over medium heat for a minute or so without browning, then add a glass of water and put on the lid. Cook for 4 to 5 minutes, until turnips are just tender. Add the greens and cook for 2 minutes more.

Rhubarb Kumquat Compote

Growing up, we'd usually have a dish of applesauce next to our dinner plates, or sometimes rhubarb stewed with sugar. But that's not the rhubarb I crave. I want my rhubarb roasted, preserving the intensity of its flavor. Kumquats are a spirited turn on the traditional orange companion.

Serve the rhubarb with plenty of sauce and a dab of Crème Fraîche (page 41) or a scoop of vanilla ice cream, or layer it with Barely Whipped Cream (page 69) to make a fool or a trifle. The compote is also good with plain whole-milk yogurt.

2 pounds rhubarb

12 kumquats, sliced

1 cup sugar

Preheat the oven to 350°F. Trim and destring the rhubarb, then cut into 4-inch batons. Put the rhubarb and kumquats in a bowl and mix well with the sugar. Transfer the mixture to a shallow baking dish. Bake for about 45 minutes, until the rhubarb is soft and suspended in a beautiful rose-hued sauce. Cool to room temperature.

summer menus

menu seven   TOO DARNED HOT, ALORS!
Provençal Toasts
Melon and Figs with Prosciutto and Mint
Deconstructed Salade Niçoise
Lavender Honey Ice Cream

menu eight   SLIGHTLY ALL-AMERICAN
Sliced Tomatoes with Sea Salt
Grilled Chicken Breasts
Corn, Squash, and Beans with Jalapeño Butter
Blueberry-Blackberry Crumble

menu nine   YELLOW HUNGER
Shaved Summer Squash with Squash Blossoms
Grilled Halibut with Indian Spices and Yellow Tomatoes
Peaches in Wine

menu ten   FEELING ITALIAN, PART I
Cherry Tomato Crostini with Ricotta
Roast Pork Loin Porchetta-Style
Fresh Shell Beans with Sage and Garlic
Nectarine and Raspberry Macedonia

menu eleven   VIVA FISH TACOS
Homemade Tortilla Chips
Fresh Tomato Salsa
Green Cilantro and Tomatillo Salsa
Avocado Salad
Fish Tacos with Shredded Cabbage and Lime

menu twelve   HOT DAY, COLD CHICKEN
Cold Pink Borscht in a Glass
Jellied Chicken Terrine
Turnip Pickles
Cherry-Almond Clafoutis

too darned hot, alors!

Provençal Toasts

Melon and Figs with Prosciutto and Mint

Deconstructed Salade Niçoise

Lavender Honey Ice Cream

I didn't make the obligatory pilgrimage to Europe straight out of college. Instead, I went to French films, cultivated European friends, and read every Mediterranean cookbook I could find. The writings of Richard Olney (another American transplant) provided a kind of inspiration for my generation of cooks, and it was easy to see why he wanted to live in Provence.

My European friends seemed to share a sense of the table that felt normal to me. The simple white cloth, the bottle of wine, the ancient ladle that served the soup. I was drawn to the idea that the experience of dining is an end in itself—so very different from pretentious American restaurants that claimed European inspiration.

I began to cook and gather friends at table the way my European friends did. When I finally did get to Europe, I'd been running the café at Chez Panisse for a few years and cooking in the Provençal spirit. Instead of giving me a raise, Alice had sent me to the South of France for three months, armed with her list of people to contact. There I met three cooks, each with a style (and lesson) of her own.

With Lulu, I sensed immediately a down-to-earth grace, generosity, true joie de vivre. On my visit to her old family vineyard in Bandol, she apologized that we weren't eating outside, where any normal person would want to be, but there was the mistral: it was too windy. We did have a glass of their Domaine Tempier rosé in the garden where her son was readying the fire for quail.

Even inside that old formal Provençal dining room, with Lulu's grandmother's great armoire, the meal felt as easy as if we were eating outdoors. First came a salad of yellow roasted peppers and rice, then the grilled quail with herbs, and then local goat cheeses and, later, an apple tart. The meal went on for hours, filled with lively stories and the spirited bonhomie of friends who hadn't been together in a while. I brought away Lulu's idea of a fine and relaxed table.

With Martine, lunch began with a trip to the little street market in Vence on a brilliant sunny day. Everything I'd read about in my Provençal cookbooks was there—eggplants, tomatoes, peppers—but little round squash too, and more olives than I'd ever seen.

Martine's house was surrounded by fig trees and the air was sweet with the scent of ripe figs. The big garden had many places to linger—wicker chairs for aperitifs, old tables tucked in leafy spots for easy lunches. Late morning, while the house was still cool, Martine made toast. Little Provençal toasts, some with tapenade, some with eggplant. She sliced some home-cured air-dried duck breast and set out a little bowl of radishes and another of olives. Melon, green salad, grilled fish, and those figs. That was it. And that's what I took from Martine.

Nathalie, who lived then in an old farmhouse in the Lubéron, took me all over in search of the best food from local artisans: *pieds-et-paquets,* braised lamb trotters with tripe from her butcher, or perhaps, fresh green tapenade with almonds from a local olive grower. Between trips to the region's many flea markets, we'd hunt out the tastiest local goat cheeses and sausages.

Nathalie understood the art of the long braise. I learned to make her stellar Provençal daube in a clay pot, simmered in a low oven for hours: beef, eggplant, mushrooms, a touch of tomato, and, in a typical Nathalie gesture, some sprigs of the rosemary she knew to grow on the nearby grave of Albert Camus.

Provençal Toasts

The traditional hors d'oeuvre in Provence is a crust of toasted bread smeared with a dab of a tasty spread. The idea is to offer your guests a little something before the meal, but nothing too filling. A bowl of olives is de rigueur, and a platter of these savory croutons (or toasts or crostini) is suitably casual.

Day-old baguettes are a staple in most Provençal kitchens, and there, as in the rest of the Mediterranean, old bread is always put to good use. Of course, it's possible to use fresh bread, but day-old works better. To make the toasts, simply slice a baguette as thin as possible. Paint the slices—an average baguette will yield about 20 slices—very lightly with olive oil, spread them in one layer on a baking sheet, and bake at 375°F until barely browned, about 10 minutes. Cool the toasts to room temperature.

Any number of savory pastes (such as the three that follow) can be used to top the toasts. Traditional favorites include anchoïade, a garlicky anchovy paste, and tapenade, a black and green olive paste. Other choices are goat cheese with herbs, roasted pepper puree, or basil pesto. All can be made a day ahead.

Then, just before serving, the toasts are spread quite lightly with the topping, just a soupçon—a scant teaspoon per toast.

tapenade

This is the simplest olive paste. For a version with more complex flavors, see Olive Relish (page 66).

1 cup pitted Niçoise olives
2 anchovy fillets, well rinsed
2 garlic cloves, chopped

½ cup olive oil, or a little more
Salt and pepper to taste

Grind all the ingredients to a fine paste in a blender or food processor. Scrape the paste into a bowl, taste, and adjust the seasoning. Thin with a little more olive oil if you like.

grilled eggplant paste

Grilling the eggplant gives this spread a faint smoky flavor.

6 Japanese eggplants
Salt and pepper
Juice of 1 small lemon
2 teaspoons chopped capers

1 garlic clove, smashed to a paste
   with a little salt
2 teaspoons chopped parsley
2 teaspoons finely minced chives
¼ cup olive oil

Put the eggplants under the broiler, over an open flame, or over hot coals and cook for 10 minutes or so, turning frequently, until the skins are blackened and the flesh is soft. Set aside to cool.

Cut the eggplants lengthwise in half and scrape the flesh from the skins. Chop the eggplant flesh coarsely with a knife and put it in a bowl. Pour off or blot any juices, and season with salt and pepper. Add the lemon juice, capers, garlic, parsley, and chives. Stir in the olive oil with a fork and mash everything a bit. Taste and adjust the seasoning.

spicy walnut paste

This walnut paste is of Arabic origin but it works well in a Provençal context.

1 small tomato, peeled and chopped
1½ cups shelled walnuts
Salt and pepper to taste
½ teaspoon cayenne or hot red pepper
   flakes or piment d'Espelette

1 garlic clove, chopped
¼ cup olive oil, or a little more

Grind all the ingredients to a paste in a blender or food processor. Put the paste in a bowl. Taste and adjust the seasoning, adding a little more oil if necessary.

Melon and Figs with Prosciutto and Mint

This easy first course depends entirely upon the quality of the fruit. Rely on the expertise of growers at farm stands or farmers' markets. Look for truly ripe, firm, locally grown melons like cantaloupe, honeydew, Charentais, or Crenshaw. Search out figs—Black Mission, Adriatic, or Kadota—that are soft to the touch, promising fruit that is juicy and sweet. A firm unripe fig will be neither.

2 or 3 ripe melons   12 slices prosciutto
24 ripe figs   A few mint sprigs

Halve the melons and remove the seeds. Slice into thin wedges, then remove the skin with a paring knife. Lay the melon slices in the center of a large platter.

Cut the figs in half and arrange them over the melons. Surround with the prosciutto. Just before serving, cut the mint leaves into ribbons and scatter the mint over the platter.

Deconstructed Salade Niçoise

It has been said that the three ingredients required for a true salade Niçoise are potatoes, green beans, and anchovies, but this salad has evolved to include tomatoes, tuna, and peppers and any number of other "creative" touches. Beware of ordering one in a restaurant—all manner of culinary travesties are routinely committed in the name of salade Niçoise, even in France.

Classically, the components are all dressed together. Here I've segregated the ingredients and piled them onto colorful platters, all the better to show off their individual glories. They'll reconnect on each diner's plate. Everything for this salad can be prepared several hours ahead of serving and kept at cool room temperature. Now all you need is a well-shaded table and lots of chilled rosé.

2 pounds small green beans, topped and tailed

4 pounds tiny new potatoes

4 pounds ripe tomatoes of different colors

2 sweet red peppers, cored, seeded, and thinly sliced

2 sweet yellow peppers, cored, seeded, and thinly sliced

4 pounds tuna steaks, 2 inches thick

Salt and pepper

2 teaspoons crushed fennel seeds

Olive oil

Basil Vinaigrette (recipe follows)

6 Soft-Center Hard-Cooked Eggs (page 154)

12 anchovy fillets (see page 172)

Green or purple basil leaves

Aïoli (recipe follows)

Boil the green beans in salted water for 5 minutes or so, until just tender. Drain and spread them out on a kitchen towel to cool.

Boil the new potatoes in salted water for 12 to 15 minutes, until tender. Let cool, then cut into halves.

Cut the tomatoes into wedges and put them in a bowl. Add the sliced peppers and set aside.

Season the tuna with salt, pepper, and the crushed fennel seeds. Drizzle with a little olive oil. Grill over coals, or sear in a hot cast-iron pan, for about 3 minutes per side, keeping the tuna on the rare side. Set the tuna aside to cool. (Or you can cook the tuna just before serving so it's still a bit warm.)

To serve the salad, season the green beans with salt and pepper, dress lightly with a few spoonfuls of the basil vinaigrette, and pile onto a platter. Cut the eggs in half, season with salt and pepper, and drape an anchovy fillet over each one. Surround the beans with the eggs. Season the peppers and tomatoes with salt and pepper, add a few spoonfuls of basil vinaigrette, and mix gently, then put them in a shallow serving bowl or on a platter.

Pile the new potatoes on another platter, sprinkle with salt and pepper, and drizzle with a little vinaigrette. Cut the tuna into thick diagonal slices or break into rough pieces and arrange alongside.

Decorate all the platters with basil leaves. Pass the aïoli separately.

serves 8–10

basil vinaigrette

This dressing is good for greens and perfect for tomato salads too.

2 shallots, finely diced
2 garlic cloves, smashed to a paste
   with a little salt
3 to 4 tablespoons red wine vinegar

Salt and pepper
A small handful of basil leaves
1½ cups olive oil

Put the shallots and garlic in the red wine vinegar, adding a little salt and pepper. Crush the basil leaves and add them. Macerate for 10 to 15 minutes.

Whisk the olive oil into the vinegar mixture. Taste and adjust the seasoning. Let the sauce stand for half an hour, then remove the basil leaves. Use the vinaigrette within a few hours.

aïoli

Aïoli, handmade garlic mayonnaise, is the wonderful, classic Provençal sauce based on garlic, olive oil, and fresh egg yolks. Other Mediterranean garlic sauces, like the Spanish allioli and the Greek skordalia, are closely related.

I might sound like a purist snob, but I really must deflate the many myths about aïoli: For one, adding other ingredients like dried tomatoes, wasabi, and the like may make a tasty sauce, but you just can't call it "aïoli." Flavored mayonnaise can contain garlic, but true aïoli contains no seasoning *but* garlic. If you add garlic to store-bought mayonnaise, you will not reproduce aïoli's fresh flavor. Another myth is that aïoli will keep for a few days. Not true. The fresh garlic flavor dissipates rapidly; aïoli must be eaten within a few hours. And, yes, you *can* make aïoli with a handheld electric beater, just be careful not to whip too much air into it.

For the best aïoli, use an extra virgin olive oil that is neither too peppery nor too strong. Try to find a fruity Provençal oil or use a mild Tuscan or California oil.

2 large organic egg yolks
2 to 2½ cups olive oil

4 to 6 garlic cloves, smashed to a paste
   with a little salt
Salt and pepper

Have all the ingredients at room temperature. Put the egg yolks in a bowl and stir with a wire whisk for a minute or so until they thicken slightly. Add a spoonful of oil at a time, whisking well as an emulsion begins to form. Be sure to incorporate the oil completely after each addition to prevent the emulsion from breaking.

Once you've incorporated half a cup of oil and the sauce is thickening nicely, continue to whisk in the oil at a more rapid pace. When the sauce becomes too thick, add a tablespoon of water to thin it, and then continue adding the oil, thinning again with water as necessary. The finished sauce should be about as thick as softly whipped cream.

Stir in the garlic, and add a good pinch of salt and a little freshly ground pepper. Let the aïoli stand for a few minutes, then stir well and taste for salt. Refrigerate the sauce, and use within a few hours.

Lavender Honey Ice Cream

Herbs grow wild all over Provence, but lavender is typically cultivated in those long lush rows you see in photographs. Provençal bees make lavender honey, and if you're lucky enough to find a jar, use it in this recipe.

2 cups whole milk

1 tablespoon lavender blossoms,
   fresh or dried

1 cup heavy cream or Crème Fraîche
   (page 41)

1 cup honey

6 large organic egg yolks

½ teaspoon salt

In a stainless steel pan, warm the milk to just under a boil. Turn off the heat and add the lavender. Let steep for 15 minutes or so, until the milk has a faint lavender flavor.

Strain the milk and return it to the pan. Add the cream and honey and warm gently.

Beat the egg yolks with the salt in a small bowl. Gradually whisk in 1 cup of the warm milk mixture to temper the yolks, then add the contents of the bowl to the pan. Cook gently for 5 minutes or so, stirring diligently, until the mixture thickens slightly.

Strain this thin custard into a large bowl and cool. Chill in the refrigerator.

Freeze the custard in an ice cream maker. There's an ideal temperature for ice cream—you want it to firm up after it's done, but not freeze solid. So transfer it to the freezer for just a little while, then serve (or store it in the freezer and leave it out to temper before serving).

slightly all-american

Sliced Tomatoes with Sea Salt

Grilled Chicken Breasts

Corn, Squash, and Beans with Jalapeño Butter

Blueberry-Blackberry Crumble

Josephine is a card shark with a wicked sense of humor. She is also a wonderful self-taught cook with an intuitive sense of how to make simple, delicious food. Spending time on a ranch in the California Sierra Mountains where she cooked, I would often tell Josephine that I'd enjoyed the meal. She'd reply, "It's nothing fancy. I'm just a salt and pepper cook."

Maybe. But she could make a mean pot of pinto beans and whip up a batch of perfect corn bread. Cooking three meals a day for hungry ranch hands is a thankless task; most ranch cooks get more gripes than compliments. But Jo charmed everyone with honest, wholesome, real food—all-American food—like good pot roast, vegetables from the garden, hot Parker House rolls, fruit pies, and cinnamon buns from scratch. Everything was completely delicious, full of flavor, perfectly seasoned. To the good ingredients on hand, Josephine added her calm common sense, her sure-footed experience—and salt and pepper.

Salt and pepper are truly essential to good cooking. Do this: Take a peppercorn and give it a little chew, then leave it on your tongue for a moment. First

you get warmth, and a bit of numbing, but soon a rounder, zestier flavor comes through. From the inside, you taste spiciness; the black outer layer is earthier. What a complex collection of flavors in one tiny peppercorn! Does freshly ground pepper really make a difference? You've just proven it does.

White and green peppercorns have very distinct flavors too, and they really cannot be used interchangeably with black pepper. Although all peppercorns grow on the same vines, they're harvested and treated differently. White pepper (the ripe inside of the peppercorn) has a very particular intensity. The French use it in white sauces so it will not show, but I like black pepper in white sauces: it might show, but it will not overpower. Green pepper tastes, well, green to me (which makes sense, because green peppercorns are harvested as immature berries). It should be used only when you want that very greenness, say in some Asian dishes.

There's a great brouhaha about salt these days, and some of it is justifiable. Expensive artisanal sea salt is naturally produced, unrefined, and high in minerals and flavor. There are many kinds to choose from. In the United States, high-quality sea salt is produced in California and Maine. Natural sea salt is mined in Utah, and then there's red sea salt from Hawaii. French sea salt is widely touted, especially fleur de sel, as is the lovely, flaky English Maldon salt.

But no matter which salt you prefer, I believe it's more important to settle on one particular kind of salt and use it for all general seasoning. Otherwise there's the danger of over- or under-salting if you keep switching, because some salts really are saltier than others. You might discover some wonderful salt in France (for a pretty Euro), but that doesn't mean there's not great salt anywhere else. I don't like the flavor of iodized salt, and I prefer coarser than finer, so I like additive-free kosher salt as an inexpensive, easily found alternative to refined iodized table salt. I save the artisanal stuff to sprinkle at the table.

Sliced Tomatoes with Sea Salt

This isn't so much a recipe as a way to think about tomatoes. Those glorious heirloom varieties in an impossible rainbow of colors that have enlivened farmers' markets in the past few years can enliven the dinner table too. You need sweet, ripe summer tomatoes for the dish to succeed. Make sure you never refrigerate tomatoes—store and serve them at room temperature.

You want 4 pounds ripe summer tomatoes, different colors if possible. Choose heirlooms such as Green Zebra, Brandywine, Yellow Taxi, Mortgage Lifter, Cherokee Purple, and Lemon Boy. Herbs—basil, chives, or parsley—are optional.

Wash the tomatoes and remove their cores with the twist of a paring knife. Slice the tomatoes about ½ inch thick with a serrated knife.

Arrange the tomato slices on a large platter. Scatter torn basil leaves, chopped chives, or slivered parsley over the top, if you wish. Just before serving, sprinkle sea salt lightly over the tomatoes, or pass a bowl of sea salt at the table.

I grilled chicken breasts recently and they turned out well. Why, my friends wanted to know, aren't they dry? The answer was simple enough. I used good-quality free-range chicken breasts. But, more important, I cooked them properly, which is to say I took them off the grill at just the right moment. The chicken breasts were at cool room temperature before I cooked them. I seasoned them with only salt and pepper, a little olive oil, and fresh rosemary. The fire was the right temperature (not too hot). The mistake most cooks make is grilling over a fire that is too hot, so they're scorching instead of cooking.

I put the breasts skin side down on the grill, let them brown slowly, and took care not to burn them. Then I turned them over and grilled them only another couple of minutes. "Treat them like a roast," I said. "Let them rest a few minutes on a platter, and they will be moist and juicy." Then I sliced them on a thick diagonal.

It's a good idea to flatten the breasts a bit so they'll cook evenly.

The best grilled chicken salad uses the same technique: Let the grilled breasts cool, but don't let them get cold. When they're still barely warm, slice them and dress with a vinaigrette, then toss quickly with tender spicy greens like arugula or young mustard greens.

Grilled Chicken Breasts

Buy organically raised, free-range chicken from a good butcher or natural foods grocery.

10 boneless chicken breast halves with skin, about 6 ounces each

Olive oil

Salt and pepper

A few rosemary sprigs

Remove the tenderloins from the chicken breasts and reserve for another purpose. With a sharp knife, trim the breasts of extraneous fat, leaving the skin intact. Place the breasts between two sheets of plastic wrap or waxed paper and flatten them a bit with a mallet or meat pounder.

Lay the breasts on a baking sheet and drizzle with a little olive oil. Season the chicken breasts on both sides with salt and pepper. Strip the leaves from the rosemary sprigs, chop them roughly, and sprinkle over the breasts. Let them rest at cool room temperature for up to an hour (or refrigerate for several hours and bring to room temperature before cooking).

Prepare a fire in a charcoal grill. When the coals are hot, set the grilling rack over them and let it heat. Be sure the rack is not too close to the coals and that the heat is not too fierce. The heat level should be that of a medium-hot sauté pan. A beefsteak can take higher heat, but for chicken, the heat must be gentler.

Lay the chicken breasts skin side down on the grill. Let them cook for about 6 minutes, until the skin is golden and crisp. Turn them over and cook for 2 minutes more. Remove the breasts to a warmed platter and let them rest for 5 to 8 minutes before serving. Carve them into thick diagonal slices.   *serves 8–10*

Corn, Squash, and Beans with Jalapeño Butter

Use this recipe as a guide, incorporating other summer vegetables such as okra, wax beans, snap peas, and sweet peppers. The jalapeño butter is also divine on corn on the cob.

2 tablespoons olive oil

1 large onion, finely diced

2 garlic cloves, smashed to a paste with a little salt

4 cups corn kernels (from 8 ears fresh sweet corn)

2 pounds summer squash or zucchini, green and yellow, in medium dice

2 pounds small green beans, topped and tailed, in ½-inch cut pieces

Salt and pepper

Jalapeño Butter (recipe follows)

Cilantro leaves (optional)

Heat the olive oil in a large heavy-bottomed pan over a medium flame. Add the diced onion and let it cook for 5 minutes or so, until softened.

Add the garlic, corn kernels, summer squash, and green beans. Season well with salt and pepper. Increase the heat to high, and cook, stirring well, for a minute or two. Add a cup of water and cover the pan. Cook the vegetables for 5 to 7 minutes, stirring once or twice. When they are cooked to your liking—soft, but not too soft—add some jalapeño butter and mix it in gently.

Serve in a warmed bowl, topped with chopped cilantro, if you wish.

jalapeño butter

Put a stick of softened butter in a small bowl. With a wooden spoon, stir in 1 minced jalapeño pepper (remove the seeds before chopping for a less spicy butter). Add salt and pepper, the grated zest and juice of 1 lime, and a tablespoon of slivered chives. Mix well.

Blueberry-Blackberry Crumble

This humble dessert is made velvety by the blueberries, which thicken the sauce. You can also use other berries, such as raspberries, loganberries, boysenberries, or olallieberries, or use all blueberries. Serve with vanilla ice cream, Crème Fraîche (page 41), or Barely Whipped Cream (page 69).

1½ cups all-purpose flour

1 cup packed brown sugar

½ teaspoon cinnamon

8 tablespoons (1 stick) cold sweet
   butter, in small pieces

3 pints blueberries

3 pints blackberries

½ cup granulated sugar

Preheat oven to 350°F. To make the topping, combine the flour, brown sugar, and cinnamon in a bowl. Add the butter and work it in with your fingertips until you have a crumbly mixture.

In another bowl, toss the blueberries and blackberries with the granulated sugar. Pile the sugared fruit into a large gratin dish or two pie plates. Mound the topping over the fruit.

Bake for an hour, or until the topping is nicely browned. Cool for 15 minutes before serving, or serve at room temperature.

yellow hunger

Shaved Summer Squash with Squash Blossoms

Grilled Halibut with Indian Spices and Yellow Tomatoes

Peaches in Wine

This is a book of recipes and menus, but I hope what it is, too, is a book about cooking by instinct—improvisational, the sort of cooking that doesn't *need* a recipe. Take zucchini. Take it, please. I know, it's the summer garden's little joke: too much, too big, not funny. Or is it?

Say you cut up an onion. Stew it slowly, salted lightly, in plenty of olive oil. Chop a zucchini or three—yellow or green, any size is fine, cubes are good. Add salt and garlic and a little red chile and simmer slowly over moderate heat until the squash is tender and juicy.

You can serve this simple concoction in a surprising number of ways: for a first course as a sort of soup, sprinkled with good olive oil and fresh chopped herbs; in an open-faced sandwich, with ricotta salata or mild feta and hot pepper; as an accompaniment to simply cooked fish or chicken. Or turn it into a wonderful pasta sauce: Stir the hot squash into soft, wide pappardelle or giant shells, with a good spoonful of fresh ricotta, a fistful of grated Parmigiano, and freshly ground pepper.

Or make a huge pancake of yellow and green zucchini, crisp and savory— it's a sight to behold. Pick your zucchini, and while you're out there, grab some

parsley, oregano, chives, whatever, and lots of basil. Julienne or grate 6 to 8 zucchini. Put in a bowl and add salt and pepper, chopped herbs, 2 or 3 beaten eggs, and a little grated Parmigiano, or not. Heat olive oil in a well-seasoned cast-iron pan, pour in the zucchini mixture, and let it brown on one side. Flip the pancake and finish it on the stovetop, or run it under the broiler until it's puffy.

Shaved Summer Squash with Squash Blossoms

One summer day at the market, everything that appealed to me seemed to be in intense shades of yellow and gold: yellow peppers, yellow tomatoes, golden peaches, the sweetest summer squash sidling up to dewy lemon-colored squash blossoms. I began to feel a yellow hunger. This salad of yellow summer squash, sliced paper-thin and dressed with fruity olive oil, makes a fine beginning to a yellow meal.

2 pounds small yellow zucchini or
    other summer squash
Salt and pepper
Olive oil

1 lemon
12 squash blossoms
½ pound ricotta salata (or mild feta)

Rinse the zucchini and wipe dry with a kitchen towel. Cut off both ends of each one. Using a mandoline or sharp thin-bladed knife, cut the squash lengthwise into very thin slices. Put the squash into a large bowl and cover with a damp towel until you are ready to serve—it only takes a minute or two to finish the salad.

Just before serving, season the squash lightly with salt and pepper and toss gently. Drizzle with olive oil just to coat. Add the juice of half the lemon. Toss again, taste, and adjust the seasoning.

Mound the dressed squash on a platter. Tear the squash blossoms (petals only) into strips and scatter them over the salad. With a sharp vegetable peeler, shave the cheese over the platter. Serve immediately.

Grilled Halibut with Indian Spices and Yellow Tomatoes

Indian spices turn any white fish flavorful—and yellow too.

2 teaspoons cumin seeds

2 teaspoons coriander seeds

2 teaspoons fennel seeds

6 cloves

1 tablespoon turmeric

½ teaspoon cayenne

8 halibut fillets or steaks,
    about 6 ounces each

Salt and pepper

2 tablespoons olive oil

8 yellow tomatoes, in small wedges

Yogurt Sauce (recipe follows)

A handful of mint leaves

In a dry cast-iron pan, toast the cumin, coriander, fennel, and cloves over medium heat until fragrant, about 2 minutes. Transfer to a spice grinder or mortar and grind fine. Put the ground spices in a small bowl and add the turmeric and cayenne.

Lay the halibut on a baking sheet and season with salt and pepper. Drizzle with the olive oil. Sprinkle the spice mixture over the fish, then massage it in. Cover and refrigerate for up to several hours. Bring the fish to room temperature before cooking.

Prepare a fire in a charcoal grill. Grill the halibut over medium coals for 3 minutes per side, until just opaque throughout (the fish can also be cooked under the broiler, baked in a hot oven, or pan-cooked).

Arrange the halibut on a large platter and surround with the yellow tomatoes. Sprinkle the tomatoes lightly with salt. Spoon a little yogurt sauce onto each portion and pass the rest at the table. Sliver the mint leaves with a sharp knife and scatter over the platter.

serves 8

yogurt sauce

Raita—the classic Indian yogurt sauce—can be spruced up with grated radish, carrot, or cucumber, but I like this plain version.

3 cups whole-milk yogurt

1 tablespoon olive oil

2 teaspoons mustard seeds

2 teaspoons cumin seeds

3 garlic cloves, finely chopped

2 teaspoons grated ginger

1 serrano chile, finely chopped

Salt and pepper

Put the yogurt in a bowl. In a small frying pan, heat the olive oil over a medium flame. Add the mustard and cumin seeds. When the seeds begin to pop, add the garlic and let it sizzle, without browning, about 10 seconds or so.

Scrape the contents of the pan into the yogurt. Stir in the ginger and chile. Season the sauce with salt and pepper. The sauce will keep in the fridge for a day or two, but it tastes best freshly made. It also makes a good dressing for cucumber salad.

Peaches in Wine

This is *not* a cooked peach dessert, nor is it overly sweet. In the spirit of this dinner, it is pure peach and pure yellow.

8 ripe peaches

2 to 3 tablespoons sugar

1 bottle (750 ml) dry white wine or rosé

Peel the peaches with a sharp paring knife. Slice the fruit and put in a bowl. Sprinkle with the sugar and toss gently. Pour the wine over the fruit, cover, and refrigerate for several hours.

To serve, spoon the peach slices into shallow bowls or glasses, adding half a cup of the winey juices to each.

feeling italian, part I

Cherry Tomato Crostini with Ricotta

Roast Pork Loin Porchetta-Style

Fresh Shell Beans with Sage and Garlic

Nectarine and Raspberry Macedonia

All over Italy you can buy *porchetta*—the national treat of roast suckling pig seasoned with wild fennel and rosemary, black pepper, and garlic—from vendors in special stainless steel trucks, fitted out with selling counters, that travel from town to town and park in markets or piazzas, just like old-fashioned ice cream vans. To my mind, snacking on porchetta with a little glass of wine is a far better thing than Mister Softee.

Often two or three porchetta trucks may be parked at the same spot. Invariably, there will be a longer line at one of them, for obvious reasons. When you get to the window, you're asked if you want the porchetta sliced from the fat end or the lean—and, of course, the fat end is the best. You always have to buy more than you need, because it's hard to get home without eating some along the way, especially the crispy skin. Porchetta is delicious warm, but perhaps even better room temperature or cold.

The pigs on those porchetta trucks are not exactly suckling age (which would be a bit below twenty pounds), they're usually larger. If you can get a small

suckling pig, it's easy to roast it in your oven or on a spit in the back yard. That's about as close as you can get to a pig on wheels here.

But you needn't have a whole pig to replicate the experience. A pork shoulder, loin, or leg seasoned properly—that is to say generously, not holding back on salt, pepper, garlic, or herbs, and left to cure overnight—will make delicious porchetta. It's most important to track down the best-quality farm-raised pork and, thankfully, farmers are once again breeding pigs that taste like pigs, concentrating on flavor (which includes some fat), not on producing that tasteless "other" white meat.

Cherry Tomato Crostini with Ricotta

Choose sweet, ripe cherry tomatoes—of different colors if possible. Sweet 100s, Ida Gold, Red Currant, Sun Gold, and Green Grape are names to look for. Also search out interesting basils, such as purple-hued opal, piccolo fino, or Greek bush, in addition to the familiar big-leaved Genovese basil. Try to get good fresh ricotta from an Italian deli or specialty cheese shop. The supermarket variety is a watered-down version of the real thing.

1 large shallot, finely diced

2 tablespoons red wine vinegar

Salt and pepper

½ cup olive oil

2 garlic cloves, smashed to a paste with a little salt, plus another peeled garlic clove or two

2 pounds cherry tomatoes, halved

1 loaf Italian ciabatta

½ pound fresh ricotta

1 teaspoon red pepper flakes

A handful of basil leaves

In a medium bowl, macerate the shallot in the red wine vinegar with a little salt. After a few minutes, whisk in the olive oil. Add the pounded garlic and the cherry tomatoes, season well with salt and pepper, and toss gently. Leave to marinate for a few minutes.

Cut the ciabatta into ½-inch slices. Spread the slices on a baking sheet and toast on both sides under the broiler until golden. Swipe the toasts very lightly with a peeled garlic clove. Don't push too hard on the garlic—you want the bread to have just a hint of garlic flavor.

Spread a tablespoon of fresh ricotta on each toast, then put them on a platter. Sprinkle with a little salt and a little red pepper. Spoon the marinated cherry tomatoes over the toasts. Sliver or tear the basil leaves and strew over the crostini.

Because it's available in our supermarkets year-round, we tend to forget that garlic, like tomatoes, has a season, and that season is summer. Of course, you cook with garlic all year, but summer's the time to let new-crop garlic's sweetness shine. Winter's sprouty garlic should be used in smaller quantities and is far better cooked.

I never understand why people think peeling garlic is such a big deal. Run from that prechopped garlic in a jar or those prepeeled cloves in containers—it all tastes old, oxidized, and rank. It's so easy to do it right. Hold a firm, fresh garlic clove top to bottom between your thumb and forefinger and quickly squeeze the clove until the skin pops. Then the clove is easily peeled. It's the same idea as smashing the unpeeled clove under the blade of a knife, but this way the clove isn't bruised until you're ready to chop it.

You don't need a garlic press or any other fancy garlic gadgets. If you have a mortar and pestle, use that for pureeing, but you don't really need one to smash garlic to a paste. Here are three tricks:

1. The French grandmother's fork method: Press the tines of a fork against a cutting board. Then rub a garlic clove back and forth over the tines to make a quick garlic paste.

2. Thinly slice a garlic clove and sprinkle with salt. With a sideways scraping motion, mash the salted slices with the side of a large knife. The salt provides the friction to create a fine puree.

3. Or use the technique I learned years ago from a French chef: Holding the handle of a large chef's knife, turn the knife upside down, with the sharp side up. Now use the flat, dull back of the blade to crush the garlic clove to a rough puree.

Roast Pork Loin Porchetta-Style

Choose good-quality, non-factory-farmed pork, on the bone or boneless, as you prefer. What's important is to have a nice layer of fat; ask the butcher not to remove too much. If you live in an area where fennel grows wild, collect a few feathery fronds. Otherwise use the fronds from cultivated fennel.

A 6-pound pork loin roast with a ¼-inch fat cover	Salt
6 garlic cloves, sliced	Olive oil
2 teaspoons fennel seeds, crushed	Rosemary sprigs
1 tablespoon coarsely ground black pepper	Fennel fronds

Turn the pork roast upside down and insert the garlic slices into the loose flesh. Sprinkle the roast with the fennel seeds and black pepper. Season the meat generously with salt and drizzle a little olive oil over it. Strip the leaves from a rosemary sprig or two, chop them roughly, and sprinkle them over the pork. Massage the seasoning into the roast.

Line a roasting pan with rosemary sprigs and fennel fronds. Set the roast on top. Cover and refrigerate for an hour or two, or, better, overnight. Bring to room temperature before cooking.

Preheat the oven to 425°F. Roast the loin for about an hour (about 45 minutes for a boneless roast), until the internal temperature reads 130°F. For a smokier flavor, cook the roast outside over coals to the same interior temperature. Remove the roast, cover loosely with foil, and let it rest for 15 to 30 minutes before carving.   *serves 8–10*

Fresh Shell Beans with Sage and Garlic

Pork and beans is always, to me, a thrilling combination and a wonderful thing to eat year-round, but fresh shell beans are a seasonal treat not to be missed. In the South, black-eyed peas, crowder peas, and fresh limas are longtime favorites and farm stands there always have them fresh in season. More and more, fresh shell beans, such as cranberry, flageolets, and cannellini, are appearing in farmers' markets around the country. If the beans are already shucked, packed in a little bag, it's a gift. If you can't find them fresh, substitute dried heirloom beans from a recent harvest. Summer shell beans cook quickly, usually in 30 minutes or so, and have a sweet, creamy succulence.

6 pounds fresh shell beans in the pod, preferably cranberry or cannellini beans	1 bay leaf
	A few sage leaves
	6 garlic cloves, sliced
Olive oil	Salt and pepper

Shuck the beans from their pods and put them in a heavy-bottomed pot. Add water to cover by an inch or so. Add a splash of olive oil, the bay leaf, sage leaves, garlic, and a good pinch of salt. Bring to a boil, then reduce the heat to a gentle simmer. Simmer the beans for about 30 minutes, until the skins are soft and the beans are tender and creamy.

Taste the beans and add salt if necessary. Cool the beans in the broth. (The beans can be cooked several hours in advance.)

To serve, reheat the shell beans. Drain them (reserve the broth for another purpose) and put them in a warmed bowl. Grind over a little black pepper and drizzle with a little olive oil.

Nectarine and Raspberry Macedonia

Macedonia was a popular fresh fruit salad here in the fifties, but it has been a staple summer dessert in Italy forever. It can be made all summer long with a mix of ripe fruit, cut small, lightly sugared, and moistened with a bit of wine or liqueur. This version features just sweet nectarines and fragrant raspberries, but feel free to add other berries or stone fruits, grapes, or melon.

8 ripe nectarines

2 pints raspberries

Sugar

2 tablespoons grappa or framboise

2 cups dry white wine

Cut the nectarines into slices or chunks and put them in a glass serving bowl. Pick over the raspberries and add them. Sprinkle lightly with sugar (ripe summer fruit needs very little), and add the grappa and wine. Mix gently, cover, and refrigerate for several hours before serving.

viva fish tacos

Homemade Tortilla Chips

Fresh Tomato Salsa

Green Cilantro and Tomatillo Salsa

Avocado Salad

Fish Tacos with Shredded Cabbage and Lime

How do you think about a meal? For me, much depends on the weather. A few years ago, I was in Paris during a record heatwave. By eight in the morning, it was already 90 degrees; even at midnight, the sidewalks were steaming. There was no end in sight. I woke one morning from a troubled sleep somewhat perversely craving fish tacos and margaritas.

I know it was a little nutty, like being in Mexico and longing for Champagne and blini, but my heart was set on it. So, first thing, I called around and invited friends for a taco fiesta after sundown. When they asked what to bring, I replied, "Cold beer. And lots of ice." Of course, finding the ingredients for tacos in Paris presented a bit of a problem. Fortunately I knew a shop that imported handmade tortillas from Mexico: expensive, but I was in it now. I had to have them. I found a big tailpiece of white-fleshed fish and begged a bag of ice so I could get it home still fresh. I knew I could find cilantro and chiles at the Asian grocery.

My craving was not for those Southern California–style fish tacos that are just fried fish with mayonnaise. They have their fans, but I am not among them. What I fantasize about are the beachside fish tacos I used to eat in a tiny makeshift joint near Veracruz, Mexico—simple tacos completely satisfying with an ice-cold Corona—fresh-grilled fish piled into warm, floppy corn tortillas, topped with shredded cabbage instead of lettuce, because the place had no refrigeration and cabbage, unlike lettuce, did fine without it. Now I always want cabbage with my fish tacos.

Homemade Tortilla Chips

It may seem excessive to suggest making your own tortilla chips, but their flavor is so much better; most commercially made chips seem too thin, not like real tortillas. And this is the traditional way to use day-old tortillas.

12 day-old corn tortillas	Salt
2 cups peanut oil	

Slice the tortillas into 1-inch-wide ribbons. Heat the oil in a cast-iron frying pan to 375°F. Fry the tortilla strips a handful at a time until crisp and lightly golden, about 2 minutes. Drain on absorbent paper and sprinkle with salt.

Fresh Tomato Salsa

As more and more commercial salsa pours into the marketplace (heavy on pineapple and fire-roasted mangoes), there is something doubly pleasurable about just-diced onion and tomatoes carefully cut into bright squares. This salsa is spirited and delicious and tastes good on almost everything. Make it fresh and eat it within an hour or two, or it loses its crunch, like a salad that's gone wilty.

2 pounds firm ripe tomatoes,
   in ¼-inch dice
1 large sweet onion, finely diced
1 or 2 serrano chiles, finely chopped
Salt and pepper

1 small bunch parsley, leaves and
   tender stems chopped
1 small bunch cilantro, leaves and
   tender stems chopped

Put the tomatoes, onion, and chiles in a bowl. Season with salt and pepper. Add the parsley and cilantro and mix well. Taste and adjust the seasoning.

Green Cilantro and Tomatillo Salsa

This green salsa is especially good with fish. It is rather spicy, but it gets balance from the tomatillos, which add both sweetness and acidity. Look for tomatillos that are small and bright green, with fresh husks. Serve this the day it is made.

2 pounds tomatillos
1 large yellow onion, thinly sliced
2 garlic cloves, roughly chopped
3 jalapeño peppers, sliced

Salt
1 large bunch cilantro, leaves and
   tender stems chopped

Remove the husks from the tomatillos. Put the tomatillos, onion, garlic, and jalapeños in a large saucepan. Add water just to cover and a good spoonful of salt. Bring the mixture to a boil.

Pour the mixture into a shallow dish. When it's quite cool to the touch, add the chopped cilantro and puree in a blender to obtain a bright green, frothy salsa.

Pour the salsa into a serving bowl.

Avocado Salad

I prefer this avocado salad to trickier guacamoles full of extra ingredients. Look for avocados that are just ripe and a little firm. Overripe avocados can taste strong and oily. When you find that really good avocado, it needs nothing more than lime juice and salt, and maybe some scallions. Dip a chip into it, put some in a fish taco, or spread it on toast.

4 to 6 avocados	Juice of 1 to 2 limes
1 bunch scallions, finely chopped	2 bunches radishes, washed and
Salt	trimmed

Cut the avocados in half and remove the pits. Scoop out the flesh with a soupspoon and put it in a serving bowl. Add the scallions, a little salt, and the juice of 1 lime. Roughly mash all the ingredients together with a wooden spoon. Taste and adjust for salt. Add more lime juice, if needed.

Put the bowl on a platter and surround the bowl with the radishes.

Fish Tacos with Shredded Cabbage and Lime

The best fish tacos require good fresh fish, good tortillas, and good salsa. Look for freshly made corn tortillas at a Latino grocery—they are always superior to those found in supermarkets. And homemade salsa is *always* better than store-bought.

Set all the accompaniments out on the table so everyone can assemble their own taco, folding a steaming hot tortilla around a chunk of grilled fish, and adding avocado, salsa, cabbage, and lime. Have a big tub of beer on ice. For dessert, cut up a watermelon, or serve *paletas,* frozen fruit ices on a stick sold in Mexican groceries.

4 pounds halibut steaks	2 tablespoons olive oil
or snapper fillets	1 small green cabbage
Salt and pepper	Juice of 2 limes
2 teaspoons powdered mild red chile	Cilantro sprigs
2 garlic cloves, finely chopped	Lime wedges
1 teaspoon oregano	3 dozen corn tortillas

Season the fish with salt and pepper. Sprinkle over the chile, garlic, and oregano and drizzle with the olive oil. Rub the seasoning into the fish, then cover and refrigerate for 2 to 4 hours. Bring the fish to room temperature before cooking.

Shred the cabbage with a mandoline or a sharp knife and put it in a bowl. Lightly salt the cabbage and toss well. Add the lime juice, toss again, and let sit for 10 minutes or so.

Grill the fish over hot coals, or broil it, for about 3 minutes per side, until just opaque. Put the fish on a platter and surround with cilantro sprigs and lime wedges.

To warm the tortillas, heat them a half dozen at a time: If you have the grill going, spread out the tortillas and heat them well on both sides, letting them puff a little. Or keep a cast-iron griddle or comal over a steady flame in the kitchen so you can warm tortillas throughout the meal. Wrap them in a clean napkin to keep the steam in—you want them soft. *serves 8–10*

hot day, cold chicken

Cold Pink Borscht in a Glass

Jellied Chicken Terrine

Turnip Pickles

Cherry-Almond Clafoutis

I suppose you can't exactly call the chicken/egg thing a partnership, since it's not exactly consensual. The particular genius of human intervention was to capture the birds in the wild and raise them for food—first harvesting the eggs while they were plentiful, then, as the flock aged, boiling the meat for soup and other dishes. If you had a few extra eggs, you made a cake, but eggs were considered a luxury.

But what began as a brilliant and perfectly eco-friendly tradition—keeping just enough chickens around the yard to supply eggs and meat for a small family—burgeoned into the big, hellacious business of factory farms, where chickens on drugs are confined in cages, lights blazing at all hours to encourage nonstop laying. This specter of avian enslavement—which produces eggs aplenty and inexpensive but bland, flavorless fryers—is enough to turn you off commercial birds (and their eggs) forever. And it should.

Just a few years ago, the only place you could find farm-raised chickens and eggs was at a farmers' market, or on the farm. But conscientious cooks and con-

sumers have lobbied to change all that. Now even mainstream supermarkets carry healthier, natural chickens and organic eggs from "happy hens."

For me, the daily egg is a necessity. Some days, I'm convinced that sunny-side up eggs are the best; other days I want my eggs poached—perhaps for lunch in a red wine sauce.

Fried eggs have all sorts of possibilities. On a slice of bread drizzled with good olive oil, or on a plate of spicy spaghetti. Or my childhood fave, a version of egg-in-the-hole we used to call eggs James Cagney (for long-forgotten reasons), where you cut out a circle in a slice of bread with a water glass, melt some butter in a pan, lay in the bread, break an egg into the hole, then fry the thing on both sides. Or quail eggs fried and served on baguette slices with a drizzle of harissa for an hors d'oeuvre. In Italy, I was once served half a dozen fried quail eggs on creamy polenta showered with shavings of fresh white truffle. Utter extravagance. In England, I ate wild gull eggs with celery salt, collected by a licensed gull-egg forager. The yolks were a brilliant orange, and the flavor somewhere between fowl and fish (some people think duck eggs taste fishy too—others swear they make the best cakes).

For salads of every sort, the best accompaniment is a soft-centered, almost runny, hard-cooked egg.

Cold Pink Borscht in a Glass

A cold glass of borscht is a refreshing beginning to a hot-weather meal. My favorite is modeled after one at Barney Greengrass, an old Upper West Side Jewish delicatessen in New York, where pink borscht, served in a water glass, is always on the menu. The borscht can be made a day ahead. Indeed, a pitcher of borscht in the fridge can even substitute for lunch on a sweltering afternoon.

1½ pounds beets

8 cups water

2 garlic cloves, sliced

2 large shallots, sliced

1 bay leaf

1 teaspoon coriander seeds

2 or 3 cloves

½ teaspoon cayenne, or to taste

1 tablespoon sugar

2 teaspoons red wine vinegar,
  or to taste

1 tablespoon olive oil

Salt and pepper

1 cup whole-milk yogurt

Chopped dill or chives (optional)

Peel and slice the beets and put them in a large saucepan. Cover with the water and add the garlic, shallots, bay leaf, coriander, cloves, cayenne, sugar, vinegar, and olive oil. Add a good spoonful of salt. Bring to a boil, then reduce to a simmer and cook for 15 minutes, or until the beets are tender. Check the seasoning of the broth—it should be distinctly sweet-sour, peppery, and flavorful. Correct the seasoning, adding salt and cayenne if necessary and freshly ground pepper.

Puree the soup well in a blender, then strain into a large bowl. Chill in the refrigerator or over ice.

Just before serving, whisk in the yogurt. Taste and adjust the seasoning, adding a splash of vinegar if necessary. Thin with a little water to achieve the correct thickness—like a thin milk shake.

To serve, pour into small water glasses. Garnish with freshly ground pepper and, if desired, fresh dill or chives.

{ANOTHER REFRESHING BEVERAGE} SUMMER BUTTERMILK DRINK

For an ultraeasy hot-day beverage, try this: Pour cold buttermilk over a few ice cubes in a large glass. Sprinkle a little salt and freshly ground pepper on top. Crumble a few cumin seeds between your fingertips, and add the cumin and a speck of cayenne. Stir and enjoy.

Jellied Chicken Terrine

This jellied chicken is an idea based on the French classic, *jambon persillé*. Two caveats: You have to like aspic, and you have to make it the day before you serve it. Then invite friends who'll appreciate it—this is the quintessential labor of love. The upside is that once it's made, it only needs unmolding, and the meal is ready. The terrine is delicious plain, or serve it with a dab of Plain Homemade Mayonnaise (page 57), a simple vinaigrette, or Herb Vinaigrette (page 270).

5 pounds whole chicken legs
  (with thighs)
2 cups dry white wine
1 bay leaf
1 small celery stalk, plus 2 tablespoons
  finely chopped celery leaves
2 garlic cloves
1 teaspoon coriander seeds
1 teaspoon peppercorns
Salt and pepper
1 cup finely chopped flat-leaf parsley

2 teaspoons finely chopped tarragon
1 bunch scallions, slivered
1 tablespoon capers, roughly chopped
Cayenne
1 tablespoon powdered gelatin
¼ cup white wine vinegar
2 or 3 heads butter lettuce, leaves
  separated, washed, and dried
6 Soft-Center Hard-Cooked Eggs
  (recipe follows)

Remove the skin from the chicken legs. Put them in a heavy-bottomed pot with water just to cover. Add the white wine, bay leaf, celery stalk, garlic, coriander, peppercorns, and a good spoonful of salt. Bring to a boil, then reduce to a gentle simmer. Skim off and discard any surfacing fat and foam. Simmer the chicken legs until they are tender, about 30 minutes. Remove the legs and set aside to cool. Leave the broth at a low simmer.

When the legs are cool enough to handle, tear the meat from bones. Return the bones to the simmering broth and cook the broth for another 30 minutes.

Roughly chop the chicken meat and put it in a bowl. Add the parsley, chopped celery leaves, tarragon, scallions, and capers. Season with salt and pepper and a

pinch of cayenne. Mix well, and transfer to a 2-quart terrine or deep serving dish and refrigerate. Strain the broth through a fine-meshed sieve, then put it in the refrigerator to cool completely.

When the broth is completely chilled, remove any congealed fat from the surface. Pour the broth (it will be partially jelled) into a pot. Be careful not to include the sediment that has settled at the bottom. Heat to just under a simmer. Taste for salt and adjust, then turn off the heat.

Soften the gelatin in the white wine vinegar and then dissolve in the broth. Allow the broth to cool to room temperature, then ladle it over the chicken. Cover and refrigerate overnight so that the terrine sets completely.

To serve, invert the terrine onto a large platter and unmold. Surround with leaves of butter lettuce and halved or quartered hard-cooked eggs.   *serves 8–10*

soft-center hard-cooked eggs

Bring a medium saucepan of water to a boil. Lower 6 large organic eggs into the rapidly boiling water. Simmer for exactly 9 minutes. (For a slightly runny center, cook the eggs for 8 minutes.) Remove the eggs from the boiling water and plunge them into a bowl of ice water to stop the cooking.

When the eggs are cool (this doesn't take very long), tap the shells on the counter to crack them, then return the eggs to the ice water. This will allow the cold water to seep between the eggs and the shells, making the eggs easily peelable. The eggs will be firm but with a moist, soft yolk.

Turnip Pickles

These pickles are wonderful with any cold meat dishes or charcuterie. The basic version takes a week to make, but there's a quick method here too, for overnight pickles.

2 garlic cloves, sliced

1 thyme sprig

½ teaspoon dried Greek oregano

1 bay leaf

2 teaspoons coriander seeds

2 teaspoons turmeric

1 teaspoon fennel seeds

½ teaspoon red pepper flakes

2 tablespoons salt

2 cups water

½ cup cider vinegar

1 tablespoon olive oil

1 pound small turnips, scrubbed but not peeled, in small wedges

Combine the garlic, herbs and spices, salt, water, vinegar, and olive oil in a bowl. Stir to dissolve salt. Pack the turnip wedges into a clean quart jar and pour in the brine mixture. Screw on the lid. Put the jar on a shelf in the kitchen and turn it over every day for a week.

After a week, refrigerate the pickles. Use within a month.   *makes 1 quart*

{IN A HURRY} QUICK PICKLED TURNIPS

For a faster pickle, simmer the turnips in the brine for about 8 minutes, or until cooked but still firm. Cool the pickles in the brine, then refrigerate overnight before serving.

{FEELING PINK} PINK PICKLED TURNIPS

For pink pickles, add 1 small red beet, peeled and sliced, and omit the turmeric.

Cherry-Almond Clafoutis

Clafoutis follows the model of every simple European housewife's dessert: Make a batter, pour it over some fruit, bake. Cherry is the best, I think. A little kirsch accentuates the flavor of the cherries.

1 tablespoon butter

Flour for dusting the pan

2 pounds cherries, pitted

½ cup blanched whole almonds

6 large eggs

2 cups packed brown sugar

2 tablespoons all-purpose flour

1½ cups whole milk

½ teaspoon organic almond extract

Splash of kirsch

Powdered sugar

Preheat the oven to 375°F. Butter and flour a 10- or 12-inch gratin dish or large cast-iron frying pan and arrange the cherries in the bottom. Scatter the blanched almonds evenly over the cherries.

Beat the eggs with the brown sugar and flour. When the mixture is smooth, whisk in the milk. Add the almond extract and the kirsch. Pour the batter over the fruit.

Bake for 40 minutes, or until the top is nicely browned and a skewer inserted in the center comes out clean. Let cool, then dust with powdered sugar. Clafoutis tastes best at room temperature.

fall menus

feeling italian, part II

Steamed Fennel with Red Pepper Oil

Roasted Quail with Grilled Radicchio and Creamy Polenta

Italian Plum Cake

Peggy, our food-writer friend, and Christopher, an amazing food photographer, came to visit us at a little house we'd rented in Umbria. As soon as they arrived from Paris, we headed straight to the local market as usual, where we wanted to buy *everything* (always a temptation). Smitten by the bounty of the fall harvest, we wound up with only vegetables and managed a vegetarian menu that was so satisfying.

Florence fennel, bulb fennel, sweet anise, and finocchio are all names for one of my favorite vegetables. With its faintly licorice perfume, it has been popular in the Mediterranean since ancient times. In Italy in the fall, the market stands are piled high with fennel, and autumn is the best time to eat it. We came home with a basketful.

The simplest way to use fennel is to shave it paper-thin with a mandoline or sharp knife, then dress it with sea salt, good olive oil, and a few drops of lemon juice. But fennel is also very good cooked. I like to boil it in salted water and serve it warm, adding olive oil and pepper at the table. Parcooked wedges can also be grilled, or sprinkled with Parmigiano and browned under the broiler.

I made a fennel gratin in a way I'd never done before. Yet I'm now remembering Richard Olney's pumpkin gratin that uses a sprinkling of flour, so maybe all our brilliant new ideas come from somewhere. I steamed the thick-sliced fennel, layered it in a gratin dish, sprinkled it with flour as if I were making a fruit pie, drizzled it with melted butter, and moistened it with milk. I added grated Parmigiano, salt, pepper, and bread crumbs, dotted the top with butter, and baked it. It was so good, and done this way, the gratin doesn't require a béchamel. This would be a great way to do cardoons, or onions, I thought.

Peggy made a salad of puntarella, that bitter Italian green, prepared as I'd seen it done in Rome, with the stems peeled and curled in a bowl of cold water, then drained and dressed with anchovies, garlic croutons, and her special top-secret dressing.

Christopher found gorgeous artichokes and prepared them two ways: Keeping their elegant stems long and stuffing mint and garlic between the leaves, she braised some of them whole in olive oil and white wine, with more herbs and garlic, then reduced the pan juices afterward to pour over. The others she pounded flat into "flowers" and fried Roman-Jewish-style.

We sat at the table outside in the cold autumn air. An old fig tree was shedding its leaves ever so slowly. We felt very lucky.

Steamed Fennel with Red Pepper Oil

Even though warm fennel is perfectly delicious just anointed with a little olive oil, red pepper adds a welcome sharpness to the sweet anise flavor.

8 fennel bulbs
Salt and pepper
Lemon wedges

Red Pepper Oil (recipe follows)
Sea salt

Trim the fennel bulbs, reserving a few green fronds, and cut them crosswise into ½-inch slices. Put the slices into the perforated top of a large steamer and sprinkle lightly with salt and pepper. Have the water in the bottom of the steamer boiling rapidly. Set the steamer basket in place and clamp on the lid. Steam for about 8 minutes, until the fennel is cooked through but still a bit firm.

Carefully remove the fennel from the steamer and arrange on a platter. Garnish with the fennel fronds and surround with lemon wedges. Send the fennel to the table and let each person dress with the red pepper oil, lemon juice, and sea salt.

red pepper oil

Heat 1 cup of olive oil in a saucepan over a medium flame. When the oil is quite warm to the touch, stir in 1 or 2 teaspoons red pepper flakes and turn off the heat. Let the oil cool to room temperature before using. The spicy oil can be drizzled over warm vegetables or over a pizza.

Roasted Quail with Grilled Radicchio and Creamy Polenta

A platter of roasted quail and polenta makes a savory autumn Italian-style feast. Farm-raised quail are readily available, and generally of good quality, but feel free to substitute wild quail or small game hens (half a hen per person) if you prefer. The question is, how many quail per person? One plump quail satisfies restrained appetites, but three quail might be necessary for a hearty one. Two each is safe.

In poultry parlance, "semiboneless" refers to quail with their breastbones removed, wing and leg bones intact. Quail are really best eaten with the fingers. I prefer bone-in quail, all the better for nibbling. Choose semiboneless quail for your bone-wary guests, but encourage them to pick up the legs with their fingers.

16 semiboneless quail,
   about ¼ pound each

Salt and pepper

Olive oil

2 tablespoons chopped thyme leaves

2 tablespoons chopped sage leaves

6 garlic cloves, thinly sliced

16 thin slices pancetta or bacon

Creamy Polenta (recipe follows)

Oven-Grilled Radicchio
   (recipe follows)

Season each quail inside and out with salt and pepper and drizzle with a few drops of olive oil.

In a small bowl, mix together the thyme, sage, and garlic. Put a small spoonful of the mixture inside each bird. Wrap each bird with a slice of pancetta. Put in a baking dish and refrigerate the birds for up to several hours, or overnight. Bring to room temperature before cooking.

Preheat the oven to 400°F. Put the quail breast side down in a shallow roasting pan (two pans side by side is easier) and slide onto the oven's top rack.

When the birds begin to sizzle, after 8 minutes or so, turn them breast side up. Continue roasting for 10 to 12 minutes more, until the quail are nicely browned and crisp and the juices run clear when the thigh is probed with the tip of a knife.

Remove the birds from the oven and let them rest about 10 minutes, loosely covered.

Pour the polenta onto a large platter. Lay the quail on the polenta and spoon the pan juices over the birds. Surround with the grilled radicchio.   *serves 8–10*

creamy polenta

The best-tasting polenta depends on good fresh cornmeal and a certain amount of tending, though the constant stirring everyone dreads is not really necessary. Most Americans do not cook polenta long enough, so it has a disagreeable raw cornmeal taste. It's worth an hour or so of cooking for the flavor and texture that you'd never get from a box of instant polenta. Like rice, the cornmeal needs time to absorb the water and swell.

Use 4 parts water to 1 part polenta. Once made, the polenta can sit for another hour.

Bring 12 cups water to a boil in a large heavy-bottomed pot over a high flame. Add 2 teaspoons salt and 3 cups stone-ground polenta and stir well with a sturdy whisk. When the water returns to the boil and the polenta begins to thicken, after a minute or two, turn the flame to low. Continue to stir while the polenta gets its bearings. After a few minutes, it will be bubbling very gently, with the occasional ploop. Stir the polenta every 10 minutes or so. If it seems to be getting too thick, splash a little milk on top and stir it in—do this occasionally, or as necessary.

After 45 minutes or so, the polenta should be nearly cooked and ready for tasting. Spoon out a small amount on a plate and let it cool slightly—hot polenta straight from the pot is likely to burn the roof of your mouth. You're looking for a lush, corn flavor and a texture that's smooth, not grainy.

Now add salt and pepper to taste, and another splash of milk, and stir well. Cook for 15 minutes longer, then taste again. Stir in a stick of softened butter. Turn off the heat and let the polenta rest, covered, for 15 minutes before serving. Covered, it will stay warm and soft for up to an hour.

oven-grilled radicchio

For each serving, count on 2 wedges of radicchio; 4 small heads will yield 8 servings.

Peel any damaged or tough outer leaves from the radicchio. Cut into thick wedges and place in an earthenware gratin dish or shallow baking dish. Drizzle the wedges with olive oil and sprinkle with salt and pepper.

Preheat the oven to 400°F. Bake on the top shelf for 10 to 15 minutes, until well browned and nearly, but not quite, charred. The radicchio can be cooked up to several hours in advance, then reheated in the hot oven when the birds come out.

Italian Plum Cake

The Italian plums I prefer are small and dark-purple-skinned, with crisp amber flesh. They ripen at the end of summer, and they're sometimes called prune or Stanley plums (How could you not love a plum called Stanley?). I used to eat them by the bagful as a kid. They make delicious jam and wonderful tarts and pies. Here they're baked in an almond batter.

1 cup unblanched almonds
½ cup sugar, plus about ¼ cup for
   topping
⅓ cup all-purpose flour
⅛ teaspoon salt

2 large eggs
½ cup whole milk
4 tablespoons sweet butter, melted
2 pounds Italian plums, pitted and
   sliced thickly

Preheat the oven to 350°F. Butter a 10-inch tart pan or springform pan. Put the almonds and ½ cup sugar in a blender or food processor and pulse until the nuts are finely ground. Add the flour and salt and pulse once more.

Transfer the mixture to a bowl. Beat the eggs with the milk and stir in the melted butter. Add the egg mixture to the almond mixture and whisk for a minute or two until the batter is smooth.

Pour the batter into the pan and smooth with a spatula. Arrange the plum slices on top in a circular pattern. Sprinkle sugar generously over the plums. Bake for 40 to 45 minutes, until the top is golden and a paring knife inserted into the center comes out clean.

The cake is best served within a few hours of baking.

in catalonia

Tomato Bread

Fish Soup with Mussels and Chorizo

Goat Cheese with Honey

Many people think they don't like anchovies, usually because they have only tasted them straight from the tin or on a bad pizza. Even if you get the oil-packed supermarket variety, a little judicious soaking will improve their flavor. As a rule, though, the better the quality of the anchovy to begin with, the better the result. I always try to bring a few jars home when I'm traveling in anchovy territory: French anchovies from Collioure in the Languedoc-Roussillon, or any anchovies from the coastal areas of the Basque country.

If you have ever been to Barcelona, you know some of the best anchovies in the world are found there. Sweet and meaty, served everywhere, they are so beloved by the locals that the best ones are never exported. (Some superior Spanish anchovies *are* exported, though, and they can be found, for a price. They're well worth it.) It is a luxury to go into almost any Barcelona bar and find a little anchovy sandwich waiting. We don't have that pleasure here, but we do have access to salt-packed Italian anchovies, nearly as delicious.

On my first trip to Barcelona, I was traveling solo, and I decided to treat myself to a night on the town. The famous Maurice Béjart Ballet was perform-

ing, and I'd always wanted to see them. I certainly didn't speak Catalan, and my Spanish wasn't very good either. But I marched right up to the box office and asked for (I thought) the most expensive seat they had.

I purchased the ticket and was surprised at how reasonable it was. A few minutes later, I was surprised when the usher gestured for me to go outside and enter from a side door. When I showed my ticket to the next usher, he pointed toward the stairs: *"Arriba! Arriba!"* Up the stairs I climbed. And up. When I found my seat at last—a hard wooden bench behind a pillar, just inches from the ceiling—I realized without a doubt that my bad Spanish had in fact bought me the cheapest ticket. The performance was thrilling nonetheless.

Afterward, I set out in search of anchovy sandwiches. I found a place and went in; the upstairs was full of tables. On each table was a little bowl where a single goldfish swam. Locals were eating anchovy sandwiches and listening to a guitarist. There were no available chairs, so I went back down to the empty bar area.

I ordered a glass of cava and an anchovy sandwich and asked the bartender if she spoke English. "A little," she replied. I sat there alone, listening to the life and laughter from upstairs. After a while she looked at me with a certain amount of sympathy, mustered up her English, and said, "Aren't you . . . very . . . boring?"

Tomato Bread

Toasted bread rubbed with garlic and tomato, topped with anchovies and a bit of Spanish olive oil, is a traditional Catalan first course, or a great snack.

6 salt-packed anchovies or
    12 anchovy fillets in oil
12 slices good country bread
1 or 2 garlic cloves

2 large ripe tomatoes, halved
Olive oil
Salt

If you're using salt-packed anchovies, rinse them under cold water and rub off the skins and fins. Remove the fillets from each side of the skeleton, and discard the bones. Soak the fillets in a small bowl of warm water for 5 minutes, then blot on paper towels.

If using oil-packed fillets, rinse them with warm water. If they are too strong tasting, soak them in a small bowl of milk for 5 minutes, then blot on paper towels.

Toast the bread. Swipe the toasts lightly with the garlic. Rub each one with a cut side of the tomato, pressing down to make the toast look red and juicy. Lay an anchovy fillet across each toast. Arrange the toasts on a platter, drizzle with olive oil, and sprinkle lightly with salt.

Fish Soup with Mussels and Chorizo

This soup is as close as my memory can take me to a table in the sand at one of those fish shacks along the beach at Barceloneta, a little strip of beach on the harbor. Those shacks may no longer exist, but the soup prevails.

Fish soup can be a chore, even for experienced cooks. This easy full-flavored version gets a kick from chorizo and extra richness from a Catalan-style roasted pepper sauce stirred in at the end. You want the fish to flake apart and become part of the broth rather than remain in separate chunks. Any fresh white-fleshed fish will do, but I have also used well-soaked salt cod (see page 232) with great success for this recipe.

4 pounds mussels

4 pounds monkfish, in 1-inch cubes

Salt and pepper

½ teaspoon crumbled saffron

4 garlic cloves, finely chopped

1 tablespoon chopped thyme

Olive oil

3 medium onions, finely diced
   (about 3 cups)

½ pound Spanish chorizo, casings
   removed and finely diced

2 bay leaves

1 cup dry white wine

6 cups Fish Stock (recipe follows) or
   Light Chicken Stock (page 73)

Roasted Pepper Sauce (recipe follows)

1 small bunch parsley, leaves roughly
   chopped

Clean and debeard the mussels and put them in a bowl. Cover with a damp towel and refrigerate. Season the fish with salt and pepper. Sprinkle over the saffron, garlic, and thyme. Drizzle with 3 tablespoons olive oil and massage in the seasoning. Cover and refrigerate for up to several hours.

In a large heavy-bottomed soup pot, stew the onions in a little olive oil over medium heat until soft. Add the chorizo and bay leaves and cook for a few minutes more.

Add the fish and white wine and simmer for 1 minute. Add the mussels and stock and turn the heat to high. Cover and cook for about 8 minutes, stirring once or twice, until all the mussels have opened.

Stir in the roasted pepper sauce and cook for a minute more. Taste the broth and adjust the seasoning. Sprinkle over the chopped parsley and serve.

serves 8–10

simple fish stock

Fish stock is quick and easy to make. It tastes best the day it's made.

Rinse 1 pound meaty halibut (or sole or cod) bones under cold water and put them in a large pot. Add a small leek and an onion, sliced, a bay leaf, and a few peppercorns. Cover with 12 cups water and heat to just under a boil, then turn the flame to low. Skim off any rising foam and cook at a bare simmer for 20 minutes. Strain the stock and keep at room temperature.

roasted pepper sauce

Char 1 large sweet pepper over an open flame or under the broiler until the skin is blistered and black all over. When it is cool enough to handle, scrape the skin from the flesh and remove the core and seeds. In a blender or food processor, puree the roasted pepper with 1 large tomato, roughly chopped, 1 garlic clove, coarsely chopped, ½ teaspoon salt, a good pinch of cayenne, and ¼ cup olive oil. Scrape the sauce into a small bowl. The sauce can be made several hours, or even a day, in advance.

Goat Cheese with Honey

In Catalonia, mild goat cheese served with honey is called *mel i mató*. Similar cheeses, like French-style fromage blanc, fresh ricotta, Italian aged ricotta salata, and Greek manouri, are paired with fragrant honey throughout the Mediterranean. In Italy and in the Basque country, aged mountain cheeses and sharp sheep's-milk cheeses are often served with honey or preserves too.

Cheese and honey makes a perfect light finish to a meal (it's good for breakfast too). Good thick yogurt with honey makes a fine dessert as well.

The most intense flavor comes from the bees' diet—search out artisanal honey (at farmers' markets) made from the blossoms of chestnut, mesquite, orange blossom, lavender, acacia, wildflower, alfalfa, buckwheat, eucalyptus, or sage.

Assemble a luscious platter of cheese, honey, and whatever ripe table grapes are at their best.

Two 6-ounce logs mild goat cheese
Chestnut honey or other artisanal
   honey

Slice each goat cheese log into 5 pieces with a thin sharp knife or cheese wire. Arrange the cheese on a platter. Top each round with a good teaspoonful of honey.

the bean soup lunch

Salumi and Olives

Zuppa di Fagioli with Rosemary Oil

Pears and Parmigiano

Almond Biscotti

Garlic toast is one of the best things to eat. There are many ways to make it, but here is my favorite. You need, first and foremost, a good loaf of bread. Find a bakery that makes an honest loaf. For me, that means a hearth-baked bread that is made of only flour, water, yeast, and salt—a loaf with a good crust, a good texture, and the flavor of wheat. It's not important whether the loaf is whole-grain or white. Day-old bread makes especially good toast.

Then comes the question of how to toast the bread. I would try to have a fire going outside, and to rig up a grill, raking coals aside to toast bread over the cooler part. (If toasting over coals is not practical, an electric toaster or even a toaster oven is fine, if less romantic.)

Cut the bread into ½-inch-thick slices. Paint each slice lightly with good olive oil. If you have access to new-crop olive oil (Italian or Californian), your garlic toast will be even more sublime.

Grill the bread over medium-hot coals. This is not the time to become impatient: you want to attain the golden toasted color only gradually, nursing the toast

for a good 3 minutes per side. If the coals are too hot, you'll never achieve that idyllic state of toast: crisp outside and soft within. Instead, you produce the burned marshmallow of toast—blackened, charred bread that has grilled too quickly. And that would be a pity.

Only when the bread is beautifully toasted can you administer the garlic. Here is where many people go very wrong. A peeled garlic clove (or a head of garlic cut in half) must be rubbed very gently against the toast. Push too hard, and you will have grated an unpalatable amount of garlic into the bread, overwhelming that carefully achieved toasty flavor. Hold back: a very gentle swipe of garlic will suffice. Before serving, sprinkle the toast lightly with sea salt.

Another method is to toast the bread dry, then drizzle with oil, rub with garlic, and sprinkle with salt.

Salumi and Olives

Picture this still life: a worn wooden board, a knife, and a Tuscan salami. There is a simple brilliance to the Italian custom of piquing the appetite by serving thinly sliced cured meats: prosciutto, salami, and a few olives before a meal. *Basta.* Nothing fancy. Nothing filling. You're still hungry when you get to the table.

This little ritual never gets old. I could repeat it daily, not just because it's easy, and not just because it's good. Maybe it makes me feel connected to an Italian past I wish I'd had. Find an Italian food store and ask to taste different cured meats until you find what you like: finocchiona, mortadella, soppressata. Do the same with olives. With a little salumi and a couple of pounds of olives, the more artisanal the better, your pantry is stocked.

Zuppa di Fagioli with Rosemary Oil

The first cold weather wants bean soup. If possible, eat this soup outside, preferably with a little fire going, after raking leaves or chopping wood. Sometimes the soup is the whole meal: white bean soup with ham hock is especially satisfying, though if you're not thinking Italian, you could cook up a pot of pinto beans with bacon, or lentil soup with chorizo. A bean soup needs gentle cooking and cannot be rushed. Make the soup the day before you plan to serve it.

Just before serving, embellish the soup with cooked pasta (tubetti or small shells, perhaps) and wilted greens, if you like.

3 tablespoons olive oil

3 large onions, finely diced

4 garlic cloves, sliced

2 bay leaves

4 cups (2 pounds) dried white beans, preferably new-crop, picked over and rinsed

2 pounds smoked ham hocks

12 cups water

1 tablespoon fennel seeds, ground fine in a mortar or spice mill

1 teaspoon red pepper flakes

Salt and pepper

1 teaspoon Rosemary Oil (recipe follows)

Garlic toast (see page 182)

Warm the 3 tablespoons olive oil in a heavy-bottomed soup pot over medium heat. Add the diced onions and cook gently until softened, about 5 minutes. Add the garlic and bay leaves and cook for a minute more.

Add the white beans and smoked ham hocks. Cover with the water and bring to a boil. Skim off any surface foam and turn the heat to low. Simmer gently for an hour, stirring occasionally.

Add the ground fennel, red pepper flakes, and a good spoonful of salt. Continue cooking for 1 hour more, or until the beans are quite tender and the smoked pork has begun to fall apart.

Taste the soup and season with salt and pepper. Cool to room temperature, then refrigerate, uncovered, overnight.

To serve, reheat the soup over a medium flame, stirring frequently. Thin with water if it has thickened too much overnight. Check the seasoning and adjust.

Drizzle a teaspoon of rosemary oil on top of each bowl of soup. Serve with grilled garlic toast. *serves 8–10*

rosemary oil

This simple flavored oil tastes best made just before serving.

½ cup olive oil   A few rosemary sprigs

While the soup is heating, warm the olive oil in a small saucepan. Chop about a tablespoon of rosemary and stir it into the oil. Turn off the heat.

Pears and Parmigiano

There's an old Italian adage that says, essentially, that a good ripe pear with a chunk of fine Parmigiano will turn a peasant into a king—at least temporarily. It is one of those blessed combinations that really delivers flavor and pleasure.

A ripe pear can be difficult to find, however. Pears are picked underripe, and most are sold that way and need to be monitored at home for a few days. To check for ripeness, press gently on the neck of the pear. If it yields, just barely, to the pressure, it is ripe. The best-tasting pears for eating out of hand are Comice and Anjou.

Real Italian Parmigiano, Parmigiano-Reggiano, is produced only in Emilia-Romagna under strict supervision and aged for at least two years. Sweet, nutty, and grainy, it makes a delicious table cheese. Other "grana"-type cheeses, such as grana padano, may be tasty, but the real thing is worth paying for. Sitting around the table peeling pears and breaking off shards of Parmigiano is a pleasurable activity that promotes all sorts of camaraderie.

Almond Biscotti

As commercially made biscotti get increasingly bigger and less flavorful, it becomes even more important to make your own. Biscotti will keep for weeks in an airtight tin, but check on them frequently: biscotti have a way of disappearing for no apparent reason. Dunking is mandatory—in red wine, sweet wine, or coffee.

8 tablespoons (1 stick) sweet butter, softened

¾ cup sugar

2 large eggs

½ teaspoon organic almond extract

2 cups all-purpose flour

1½ teaspoons baking powder

Pinch of salt

¾ cup sliced almonds

Preheat the oven to 325°F. Using a handheld or standing mixer, cream the butter and sugar in a large bowl. Beat in the eggs and almond extract.

Mix together the flour, baking powder, and salt, then slowly incorporate into the butter mixture. Add the sliced almonds and mix for a minute more.

Put the dough on a floured board and divide it into thirds. Roll into logs about 1½ inches in diameter. Place the logs on a parchment-lined baking sheet and bake for 25 minutes, or until lightly browned. Remove the logs and let them cool slightly.

While the logs are still warm, slice them on the diagonal about ½ inch thick. Arrange the slices on two baking sheets and bake for 5 minutes, or until barely brown. Turn the biscotti over and bake for 2 to 3 minutes more. Cool on a rack.

makes 4 dozen

another early autumn

Roasted Pepper Salad

Double Duck Breast with Baked Figs and Duck Liver Toasts

Panna Cotta

One of the attractions of doing your food shopping at an outdoor market is the likelihood of encountering a vendor with a little personality or a lot of eccentricity. Such is the case in my neighborhood market in Paris, a thrice-weekly event in a small square off the Boulevard Saint-Germain. But the star of the market shows up only on Saturdays. And he shows up whenever he wants.

While other vendors are there by the crack of dawn, The Bird Man of Place Maubert wheels in about 10 A.M. and takes his time setting up, stocking his stand with the ducks, quail, pigeons, guinea hens, poussin, capon, and rabbits he's raised on a farm two hours from Paris. He has hen eggs and duck eggs, and he even hangs the occasional wild boar or young goat or deer. Then he stacks jars of pâtés and confits and gizzards and duck fat that come straight from his farm.

There's always a crowd waiting in line for him. But it's worth the wait—for the birds, sure, but also for the theater. You know you'll be standing in that line for a good long while as he prepares each client's wish: carving the breast from a fat chicken, gutting and singeing a guinea hen and tying it for roasting, skinning a wild hare and telling the customer how to cook it.

This he accomplishes with total dexterity, all the while entertaining the crowd with nonstop schtick, gestures, and grandstanding. We call him The Bird Man not just because of his beak, or the fowl that he sells, but because of the strange cacophony of squawks and screams he emits as he goes about his business, crowing like a rooster, quacking like a duck.

I take comfort in all this, knowing that when I ask him for only the breasts from three large ducks, he's ready, willing, and able. And he's sure to have customers for the legs.

Roasted Pepper Salad

This smoky, velvety salad has the color intensity of fall in all its glory, using the end-of-season's sweet peppers.

12 large sweet peppers, preferably a
    mix of yellow, orange, and red
Salt and pepper
2 garlic cloves, smashed to a paste
    with a little salt

1 tablespoon capers, rinsed
Red wine vinegar
Olive oil
½ cup Niçoise olives, rinsed
Basil leaves

Roast the peppers over an open flame, either a wood fire or on the stovetop, or under the broiler. Try to get the peppers as close to the flame as possible so their skins will blacken and blister quickly. Turn the peppers frequently with a pair of tongs so they roast evenly.

Spread the peppers on a baking sheet so they can cool to room temperature. Some cooks will tell you to cover the just-roasted peppers, or put them in a bag, but I believe too much steaming overcooks the flesh.

When the peppers are cool enough to handle, split them top to bottom with a large knife. Scrape the seeds from the insides, then turn each pepper half over and scrape away the charred skin. When all the peppers are scraped, slice them into 1-inch-wide strips and put them in a bowl. Season with salt and pepper and toss well. Add the garlic, capers, and a teaspoon or two of red wine vinegar.

Drizzle lightly with olive oil. Toss again. Don't refrigerate the peppers—it'll kill their delicate flavor. Leave the salad at room temperature until ready to serve, up to several hours.

To serve, taste and adjust the seasoning, then mound the salad on a platter. Garnish with the olives. Drizzle with a little more oil. Decorate the salad with basil leaves.

Double Duck Breast with Baked Figs and Duck Liver Toasts

Roasting a whole duck at home can be an ordeal. Instead, I use this technique—it's well worth knowing—of tying two large breasts together to make a manageable roast. The duck is roasted to a rosy hue, just past rare, then sliced. Each "roast" is enough for four, so you will have leftovers. A drizzle of sweet aged balsamic vinegar is the only sauce it needs. Leftover duck is good cold for lunch, in a salad with lightly dressed arugula and toasted walnuts.

3 tablespoons salt	6 garlic cloves, slivered
1 teaspoon peppercorns	6 large Muscovy duck breasts,
½ teaspoon allspice berries	about 1 pound each
½ teaspoon juniper berries	Baked Figs (recipe follows)
A few cloves	Duck Liver Toasts (recipe follows)
2 bay leaves	Aged balsamic vinegar

Put the salt in a small bowl. Finely grind the peppercorns, allspice, juniper, cloves, and bay leaves in a mortar or spice mill. Mix the ground spices with the salt. Add the garlic.

Trim the duck breasts and lay them on a baking sheet or platter. Season each breast on both sides with the spice mixture, massaging the seasoning into the flesh with your fingers.

Now pair up the breasts, and make each pair into a sort of sandwich—that is, stack one breast on top of the other, skin sides out. With butcher's twine, tie the "sandwiches" together, to make 3 compact little roasts. Wrap and refrigerate for at least several hours, or overnight.

Place the breasts in a shallow roasting pan and let them come to room temperature. Preheat the oven to 400°F. Pop the roasts into the oven and cook for

15 minutes. The duck will have rendered a fair amount of fat. Carefully pour off the fat (to save the fat for cooking, cool, strain, and refrigerate). Turn the roasts over and return to the oven for 15 minutes more, or until nicely browned. An instant-read thermometer should register 125°F for a succulent, rosy medium-rare.

Remove the duck from the oven and pour off any accumulated fat. Let the roasts rest for 10 or 15 minutes.

Remove the twine and cut the duck breasts crosswise into ⅛-inch-thick slices. Arrange the slices on a warmed platter, and garnish with the baked figs and liver toasts. Drizzle a little aged balsamic vinegar over the duck and the figs.   *serves 12*

baked figs

Warming a fig can enhance its essence. For the last of the season's figs, roasting helps to concentrate flavors and bring out their sweetness. Roasted figs make a fine dessert also, served with Barely Whipped Cream (page 69) or Crème Fraîche (page 41).

24 ripe figs   Olive oil
Thyme branches

With a sharp paring knife, cut the figs in half top to bottom, right through the stem, so their natural shape is preserved.

Preheat the oven to 400°F. Scatter a few thyme branches in the bottom of a shallow earthenware dish (or two) just large enough to hold the figs. Place the figs cut side up in the dish. Spoon a few drops of olive oil over them.

Bake the figs for about 20 minutes, until they puff a little and look juicy. Serve the figs on the duck platter, warm or at room temperature.

duck liver toasts

These tasty toasts—the Italians call them crostini—perfectly complement the roast duck, or they can become a first course on their own.

1½ pounds duck or chicken livers

Salt and pepper

2 tablespoons olive oil

2 slices pancetta, in small slivers

2 large shallots, finely diced

2 teaspoons chopped thyme

A splash of dry sherry or
    sherry vinegar

4 tablespoons butter, softened

1 baguette, sliced and toasted

Trim the livers, blot on paper towels, and season with salt and pepper. Heat the olive oil in a wide skillet over a medium flame. When the oil is hot, add the pancetta and shallots and cook until the shallots are nicely browned.

Add the livers and turn up the flame. Stir well and continue cooking, shaking the pan occasionally, until the livers are cooked through but still a little pink. Slice one to check. Add the thyme and sherry, and transfer the contents of the pan to a cutting board. Let cool to room temperature.

With a large knife, chop the livers with the pancetta and shallots to a rough paste, then put the paste in a small mixing bowl. Mash the butter into the paste with a wooden spoon. Taste and adjust the seasoning. Cover tightly with plastic wrap and keep at cool room temperature until ready to serve (up to 2 hours), or refrigerate and bring to room temperature before serving.

Spread on toasted baguette slices.

Panna Cotta

This silky, eggless custard is surprisingly easy to prepare.

3 cups half-and-half

1 cup Crème Fraîche (page 41)

One 2-inch piece of vanilla bean

½ cup sugar

¼ teaspoon salt

2 teaspoons powdered gelatin,
    softened in 2 tablespoons cold water

A few berries (optional)

Combine the half-and-half, crème fraîche, vanilla bean, sugar, and salt in a heavy-bottomed saucepan and warm over medium heat (do not boil). Stir to dissolve the sugar. Add the gelatin and stir well. Turn off the heat.

Fish out the vanilla bean, cut it lengthwise in half, and scrape out the seeds; add the seeds to the gelatin mixture. Cool to room temperature.

Ladle the cooled mixture into ten 4-ounce glasses or ramekins. Cover with plastic wrap. Refrigerate for at least 6 hours, or, preferably, overnight.

To serve, invert each glass over a soup plate. After a minute, wiggle the glass to unmold the panna cotta. Serve the panna cotta plain or with a few berries.

dinner for a tuscan

Green Lasagne with Greens

Bistecca with Fried Artichokes and Potatoes

Castagnaccia

My friend Tony was born in San Francisco, but his parents are from Lucca. Growing up, he spent all his summers there. Though he is American in many ways, I have to say that Tony is Italian first—especially when it comes to eating and cooking. It's fun to go to the market with him and watch him get excited, and it's even more fun to cook with him.

Tony sells real estate for a living, but he is a natural cook. Put him in front of a stove, and he's happy. Give him a couple of roasting chickens and he's in heaven, from the moment he puts them in the oven to the moment he carves them and brings them to the table. Watch him nurse a slow-cooked tomato sauce for pasta, and you know you'll be eating something special. But if you really want to get him smiling and salivating, hand him a few bunches of escarole, kale, and chard. Italians are crazy for greens, and Tony is no exception.

Satisfying, earthy cooked greens taste deeply healthy, particularly if the mixture includes some slightly bitter ones, like rapini, with its mysterious, almost-almond bittersweetness. And wild greens, like nettle, mallow, and dandelion are even better, if you know where to forage for them (as many Italians do). But even

cultivated spinach is a perfectly wonderful green: I never did understand why children are supposed to hate it. (Perhaps I was an odd child—I always loved it.)

In Italy, an abundantly satisfying antipasto is a plate of cooked greens with olive oil and lemon, served at room temperature. Its tongue-clinging, clean flavor is a refreshing way to start a meal. I love cooked-down broccoli rabe on toast or chopped greens in soup. And, of course, greens with pasta.

I thought hard about the dinner menu for Tony's birthday, and I came up with green lasagne. That way he could have two of his favorite things: his pasta and his greens. But there had to be a meat course too. Because no matter how good the pasta, I knew Tony would say afterward, "What, no meat?"

Green Lasagne with Greens

For this lasagne, I add pureed raw greens to the pasta dough and use cooked greens for the filling. I have a habit of saving greens: the outer leaves of escarole and curly endive, radish tops, young turnip tops, and oversized (or any size) arugula. All of these can be combined with spinach or chard and wilted together with olive oil, garlic, and a touch of hot pepper, then chopped roughly for a filling for lasagne or ravioli.

FOR THE PASTA
2 cups shredded raw greens—a
   mixture of chard and spinach
2 small eggs

½ teaspoon salt
2 tablespoons olive oil
3 cups all-purpose flour,
   or a little more

FOR THE FILLING

3 tablespoons olive oil

4 garlic cloves, finely chopped

1 teaspoon red pepper flakes

2 pounds chopped washed greens—
   a mixture of chard, spinach,
   and rapini (broccoli rabe)

Salt and pepper

1 pound fresh ricotta

Grated zest of ½ lemon

FOR THE BÉCHAMEL

4 tablespoons butter

¼ cup all-purpose flour

5 cups whole milk, or a little more

1 bay leaf

1 thyme sprig

Salt and pepper

Nutmeg, for grating

2 cups grated Parmigiano

To make the pasta dough, put the shredded greens, eggs, salt, and olive oil in a blender or food processor and puree until smooth. Scrape the green puree into a mixing bowl and add the flour. Knead into a soft dough. If the dough seems too sticky, sprinkle with a little more flour and knead some more. Wrap the dough in plastic and set it aside to rest.

For the filling, heat the olive oil in a large deep saucepan over a medium-high flame. Add the garlic and let it sizzle, without browning. Add the red pepper flakes, then add the greens. Stir well and let the greens wilt for a minute. Season with salt and pepper and stir again.

Now put the wilted greens in a colander to drain. When the greens are cool enough to handle, squeeze them in your hands to remove any excess liquid. Set them aside.

Put the ricotta in a bowl. Add the lemon zest, season with a little salt and pepper, and mix well.

For the béchamel sauce, melt the butter in a large heavy-bottomed saucepan over a medium flame. Stir in the flour and cook, stirring, for a minute, without letting the mixture brown. Whisk in the milk a half cup at a time, letting the sauce thicken after each addition. When all the milk has been added, add the bay leaf and thyme and season with salt and pepper.

Turn the flame to low and let the sauce cook gently for 10 minutes. Thin if necessary with a little more milk. Grate in some nutmeg. Check the seasoning and adjust. Strain the sauce into a double boiler and keep warm.

Butter a large baking dish, approximately 8 by 12 inches. Have a large pot of salted boiling water on the stove and a large bowl of cold water nearby.

Divide the dough into 3 or 4 pieces. Roll each piece into a thin sheet with a pasta machine at the next-to-thinnest setting, placing the pieces on a floured counter as you work. Cut the sheets into 8-inch lengths. Leave the pasta sheets uncovered on the floured counter.

To assemble the lasagne, boil 2 sheets of pasta at a time so they cook evenly and don't stick together. Cook the sheets as you go, for 1 minute or less, leaving them quite al dente. Plunge them immediately in the cold water to stop the cooking, then blot on a kitchen towel.

For the first layer, lay the 2 pasta sheets side by side in the bottom of the gratin dish. Arrange a quarter of the cooked greens over the pasta. Dot the greens with one-quarter of the ricotta. Spoon ½ cup béchamel sauce over the ricotta, and sprinkle with a handful (about 2 tablespoons) of Parmigiano. Repeat the process to make 3 more layers. Finish with 2 or 3 sheets of pasta on top, coat with the remaining béchamel, and sprinkle with the rest of the Parmigiano.

Refrigerate the assembled lasagne for up to several hours, or overnight to marry the flavors. Bring to room temperature before baking.

Preheat the oven to 375°F, and bake the lasagne for 30 minutes or so, until bubbling and lightly browned on top. Let rest before serving. *serves 8–10*

Bistecca with Fried Artichokes and Potatoes

Baby artichokes are the size of an egg, with no choke. After you remove a few outer leaves, the entire artichoke is edible.

4 pounds flank steak

Salt and pepper

Olive oil

4 pounds medium potatoes,
   such as Yellow Finn

2 pounds baby artichokes

1 lemon

4 garlic cloves, finely chopped

1 bunch flat-leaf parsley,
   leaves roughly chopped

½ pound arugula, washed and dried

Lemon wedges

Season the flank steak generously with salt and coarsely ground black pepper. Drizzle with a little olive oil and massage in the seasoning.

Cover and refrigerate for at least several hours, or overnight. Bring to room temperature before cooking.

Peel the potatoes and cut them into small chunks or wedges. Boil the potatoes in salted water until just done (soft when pierced with the tip of a knife). Drain the potatoes and spread them on a baking sheet to cool.

To prepare the baby artichokes, cut off the tops and remove a few outer leaves from each to reveal the pale green centers. Trim the stem ends with a paring knife. Slice the artichokes lengthwise ¼ inch thick. Put the slices in a bowl of cool water. Squeeze in the juice of the lemon.

Prepare a fire in a charcoal grill. While you wait for the grill to heat, panfry the artichokes and potatoes: Drain the artichoke slices and blot with a kitchen towel. Put a large skillet over a high flame. Add ½ inch of olive oil and let it heat. Add the artichokes and stir them around in the oil for a minute or so. Add the potatoes and let them sizzle with the artichokes.

Turn flame to medium, shaking the pan and stirring the vegetables, until they brown and crisp, about 10 minutes. Season with salt and pepper. Add the garlic and let it sizzle without browning. Stir in the parsley and turn off the heat.

Grill the flank steak over hot coals. For a rare steak, cook about 4 minutes per side, just until juices begin to appear on the surface. Transfer to a platter and let the steak rest for 10 to 15 minutes before carving.

Carve the flank steak in thin slices against the grain. Arrange the meat on a large warmed platter. Reheat the fried artichokes and potatoes if necessary and spoon around the steak. Garnish the platter with arugula leaves and lemon wedges.

serves 8–10

Castagnaccia

Castagnaccia is a rustic, traditional, not too sweet Tuscan cake made from chestnut flour. In Florence, you can find the cake in some old-fashioned trattorie, looking a bit like cracked slabs of brown earth. Chestnut flour can be purchased in many Italian markets or online.

3 cups chestnut flour

2 cups water

Olive oil

½ teaspoon salt

½ cup raisins, plumped in warm water
    and drained

¼ cup pine nuts

A few rosemary sprigs,
    leaves roughly chopped

Preheat the oven to 425°F. Put the chestnut flour in a large bowl. Whisk in the water and mix well to remove lumps. Stir in 3 tablespoons olive oil and the salt. The mixture will resemble thick pancake batter.

Grease a 12-inch cast-iron skillet generously with olive oil. Pour in the batter. Sprinkle the raisins over the batter, then the pine nuts and rosemary. Bake for 20 to 25 minutes, until the top is lightly browned and cracked. Cool slightly, then remove from pan.

The cake tastes best slightly warm.

a simple moroccan supper

Spiced Olives

Berber Pizza

Harira Soup

Orange Salad with Dates

I had dreamed of visiting Morocco ever since reading Paul Bowles's *The Sheltering Sky* as a lad. I went on to read his other novels, and his wife, Jane's, too. I picked up Paula Wolfert's definitive *Couscous and Other Good Food from Morocco* and cooked my way through that book. I was hungry.

So it was a bit disconcerting when I had a chance, at last, to visit a friend to find myself in southern Morocco during the month-long celebration of Ramadan, when Muslims must fast from sunrise till dusk and are forbidden even a sip of water. Many restaurants are closed altogether. Where was the food? I spent my days waiting for the sun to set.

At sundown, it is customary to break the fast with a nurturing soup, usually harira, made with dried fava beans, chickpeas, and lentils. We were invited to several families' houses to join in the fast-breaking. Moroccan hospitality is legendary, and we were always made to feel like part of the family. These suppers always began with mint tea and, curiously, a kind of spiced café au lait as well, and glasses of buttermilk too—all served at the same time.

Next, platters of sweets or semolina pancakes with honey were offered, along with a flatbread stuffed with a meaty onion filling, which everyone called Berber pizza. Bowls of harira soup were passed—spicy, savory, and satisfying.

Then, as we lounged on pillows and cushions, water was boiled and more mint tea was served. After an hour or so of relaxation, more dishes arrived, usually a steaming platter of couscous, piled high with chicken and vegetables. You were supposed to eat a lot at night because at sunrise the fasting would begin again. Alas, we were usually so satisfied by the delicious bread and soup, we thought we could manage only a polite taste of couscous. In truth, I forced myself to several helpings. To be extra polite, of course.

Spiced Olives

If you have a good olive merchant, you may trust his spiced olives, but it's easy and satisfying to make your own. Let the olives marinate in the spice mixture for a couple of hours. They'll keep for a week in the refrigerator.

2 cups good green olives, such as
   Picholine

2 teaspoons cumin seeds

2 teaspoons coriander seeds

2 garlic cloves, smashed to a paste with
   a little salt

1 lemon, thinly sliced

1 tablespoon paprika

½ teaspoon cayenne

½ cup olive oil

Salt

Rinse the olives and put them in a bowl.

Toast the cumin and coriander in a dry skillet over medium heat until the spices begin to color a bit. Coarsely grind in a spice mill or mortar.

Mix the olives with the cumin, coriander, garlic, lemon, paprika, cayenne, and olive oil. Sprinkle lightly with salt.

Berber Pizza

This is a thin double-crust pan bread traditionally baked on a hot griddle. I've modified the technique so it can be baked in a conventional oven.

FOR THE DOUGH
2 teaspoons active dry yeast
1¾ cups warm water
4½ cups all-purpose flour,
 or more as needed
1 teaspoon salt
⅓ cup olive oil

FOR THE FILLING
4 medium onions, thinly sliced
Olive oil

1 tablespoon butter
1 teaspoon cumin seeds,
 toasted and ground
1 teaspoon coriander seeds,
 toasted and ground
1 teaspoon powdered hot red chile
2 teaspoons paprika
2 teaspoons black pepper
Salt
2 tablespoons chopped parsley
2 tablespoons chopped cilantro

For the dough, mix the yeast, ¾ cup warm water, and ½ cup flour together in a large bowl. When the mixture is foamy and active, add 4 more cups flour, the salt, olive oil, and remaining 1 cup water. Stir to mix, then knead until smooth, adding a little flour if necessary, but aiming for a soft dough. Cover and let rest for 2 hours, refrigerated, or overnight.

 For the filling, in a large heavy skillet over high heat, wilt the onions quickly in 2 tablespoons olive oil and the butter, letting them color a bit but leaving them a little crunchy.

THE CAPSICUM PERK

I believe many Western dishes can benefit from a little chile heat—fresh or dried. Italians would not be surprised to find a few red pepper flakes in their greens. And despite the fact that no self-respecting Frenchman would agree, even a traditional French beef daube, a Gruyère omelette, or a tomato salad can be improved with a judicious bit of jalapeño.

I can't resist buying fresh chiles whenever I see them. I find it comforting to have a bowl of jalapeños nearby, especially those that look a bit like strawberries as they begin to turn red. I like thin, sharp serrano chiles and dull-hot Thai bird peppers. It's hard to resist a few shiny, dark poblanos, so good roasted and dressed with sour cream. Inevitably, though, this compulsion results in a collection of shriveled, half-dry, and dried chiles hanging around in my kitchen. But I always manage to work the semidried chiles into a braise, or a marinade. And when they're dried, I make my own chile powder (thanks to a spice grinder) without going to the store.

This penchant for chile peppers' high notes explains, too, my love for the French Basque piment d'Espelette, and the smoky Spanish Pimentón de la Vera. I also appreciate the depth and sharpness of good Hungarian paprika. A trick for adding the "capsicum perk" to a dish (without having your guests actually encounter solid bits of chile pepper) is to make a fine puree of fresh green chiles. Stir a small spoonful into, say, a mustard vinaigrette. The flavor is heightened mysteriously.

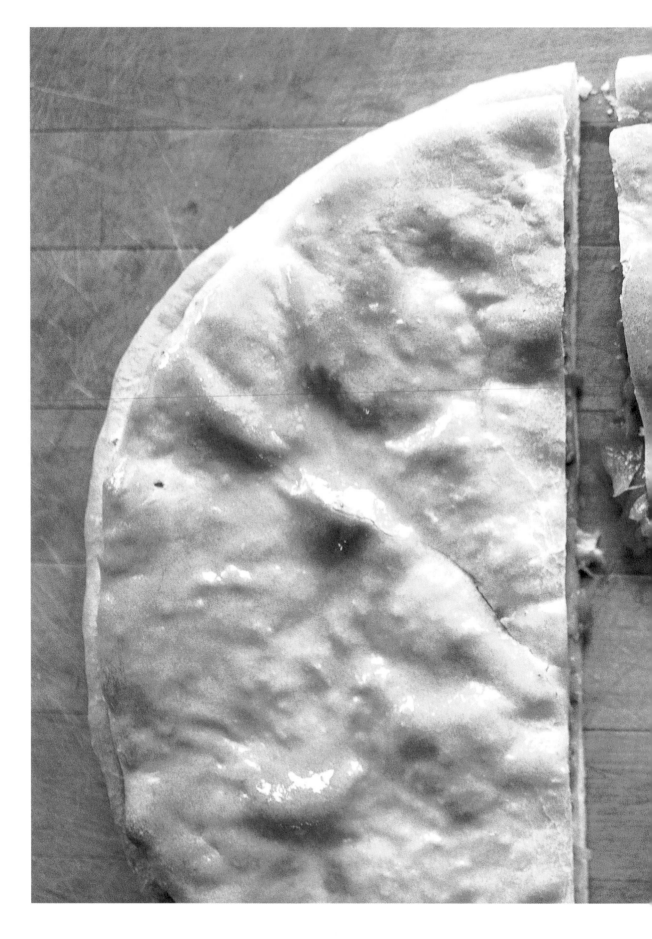

Add the cumin, coriander, red chile, paprika, and black pepper. Season well with salt. Taste and adjust the seasoning—the onions should be rather spicy. Remove the onions to a plate to cool, and sprinkle with the chopped parsley and cilantro.

Preheat the oven to 400°F. Divide the dough into six 5-ounce pieces. Knead each piece into a smooth ball. Cover with a clean towel and let the dough rest for 10 minutes.

To make the first pizza, roll out 2 dough balls into 8-inch rounds. Place one-third of the onion mixture on one of the rounds. Cover with the other round of dough. Pinch the edges together with your fingers. With the palm of your hand, press down on the package to flatten it, then roll out the filled dough to make a 12-inch circle (the onion mixture will spread inside the dough as you roll). Follow the same procedure to make 2 more pizzas.

Transfer one pizza to a lightly oiled baking sheet. Bake up to 2 pizzas at a time for 15 to 20 minutes, flipping the pizza halfway through the baking to ensure even browning. (The pizzas can be baked up to 2 hours in advance and reheated on baking sheets in a hot oven.) Paint the tops with a little olive oil and sprinkle with salt and cut into wedges just before serving.

Harira Soup

A velvety texture is the aim, and long, gentle simmering is the key. Harira must cook for a minimum of 2 hours. The soup can be made a day ahead; the flavor will only improve.

2 tablespoons olive oil

1 pound boneless lean shoulder of
    lamb, in ½-inch cubes

2 large onions, finely diced

½ teaspoon crumbled saffron

1 teaspoon *each* ginger, cinnamon,
    turmeric, and pepper

2 teaspoons powdered hot red chile

6 garlic cloves, finely chopped

1 cup dried peeled fava beans,
    picked over and washed

1 cup red lentils,
    picked over and rinsed

13 cups water

Salt

6 ripe tomatoes, coarsely chopped

1 cup coarsely chopped parsley

1 cup coarsely chopped cilantro plus
    slivered cilantro for garnish

⅓ cup all-purpose flour

4 tablespoons butter

Lemon wedges

Heat the olive oil in a deep heavy-bottomed soup pot. Brown the lamb lightly, then add the chopped onions, stir, and brown them. Add all the spices and the garlic and let them sizzle for a few minutes. Add the favas, lentils, and 12 cups water and bring to a boil. Reduce the heat to a bare simmer. Add 2 teaspoons salt and simmer, stirring occasionally, for 1 ½ hours.

Put the tomatoes, parsley, and cilantro in a blender with a little salt and puree the mixture. Add the puree to the soup and simmer for another ½ hour or so.

Now puree half the soup and return it to the pot. Make a slurry with the flour and remaining 1 cup water (stir together until smooth), add to the soup, and simmer for 10 minutes. Taste and adjust for salt and spice. Add the butter and stir until melted. The texture should be quite smooth, neither too thick nor too thin.

Ladle the soup into bowls and sprinkle with slivered cilantro. Squeeze a few drops of lemon juice into each bowl, and pass a plate of lemon wedges.

serves 8–10

Orange Salad with Dates

This is a classic Moroccan way to finish a meal. Oranges grow nearby, dates too. Every stall in the market sells them.

8 navel oranges

Sugar

1 pomegranate

Cinnamon

2 pounds dates—Medjool, Deglet Noor, Zahidi, or a mixture

Peel the oranges. Slice crosswise into ¼-inch-thick disks. Arrange in concentric circles on a platter. Sprinkle lightly with sugar.

Cut the pomegranate into quarters. Force out the seeds by inverting the skin of each quarter over a bowl. Pick out any white pith and discard. Sprinkle the pomegranate seeds over the oranges.

Sprinkle a little cinnamon over the platter. Bring the orange salad to the table with bowls of the dates.

winter menus

tapas party

Octopus Salad with Pickled Onions and Pimentón

Potato and Salt Cod Tortilla

Sea Scallops a la Plancha

Black Paella with Squid and Shrimp

Membrillo and Sheep's-Milk Cheese

Madrid spoiled me. Seville ruined me. I first met tapas in Madrid's Plaza Mayor, where a bronze statue of King Philip III on a horse hovers at twilight like a dark spirit over the enormous square bordered with tapas bars. The bars are open all day, but they don't really get going until 11 P.M. I found an appealing place and ordered a *ración* of jamon ibérico. A plate arrived, big enough to feed a tableful. I couldn't get enough of that cured ham—I finished it all.

My flamenco guitar friend, Kenny from Berkeley, told me there was one place in Seville I could always find him and that was the Bar Modesto, a place that specializes in seafood tapas like *angulas*—baby eels sizzled in olive oil. In an odd sort of cross-pollination, the restaurant had all its tapas cast in plastic in Japan, they way they do sushi. At the bar, the entire counter is an array of plastic tapas displayed in clay cazuelas.

There are just a few things appropriate to drink with tapas: chilled fino sherry, draft beer, a big Spanish red, or *tinto de verano,* the unknown and better cousin of sangria: half a glass of red wine with half a glass of sparkling water and ice. Or J&B whiskey. In Seville, the eating and drinking went on all night. You'd never want to abandon the group, so you'd habitually stay up until five.

Of course, once I was back in California, I made the somewhat predictable mistake of trying to bring that tapas culture home. I'd prepare many little plates—shrimp *a la plancha,* stuffed piquillo peppers, and *pinchos moruños,* little spicy skewers of grilled pork—to serve at parties that would begin late and last forever. I was ready to party all night, but my friends were tired by midnight and had to get up for work the next morning. But while the Spanish form didn't exactly translate, the substance did.

Small bites Spanish-style are an ingenious way to have a party and feel like a guest too. Much can be prepared ahead, ready to serve. It's free-form, really, no need to set the table, or bring things out in courses, and it doesn't really matter where you begin or where you end.

Octopus Salad with Pickled Onions and Pimentón

Octopus salad is one of the most delectable things I know. Octopus is tricky: if you let it boil, it will toughen. Simmered slowly—and I mean really slowly—in an aromatic broth, you coax it into staying tender. The meat emerges succulent and savory. Pimentón is a flavorful smoky Spanish paprika available sweet (*dulce*) or hot (*picante*); Pimentón de la Vera is the best. The octopus's inherent sweetness is offset by a drizzle of olive oil and a sprinkle of smoky pimentón.

1 medium octopus, about 3 pounds

1 bay leaf

1 thyme sprig

1 onion, halved

4 garlic cloves, sliced

1 small dried red chile

1 teaspoon coriander seeds

Extra virgin olive oil

Salt and pepper

Pimentón de la Vera, sweet or hot

Pickled Onions (recipe follows)

Rinse the octopus and, if it hasn't been cleaned, trim off the ink sac, beak, and eyes. Put it in a large pot and cover with cold water. Add the bay leaf, thyme, onion, garlic, chile, and coriander seeds. Add a splash of olive oil and a good pinch of salt. Cover the pot and bring just to a boil, then turn down the heat to low.

Simmer *slowly* for 45 minutes to an hour, never allowing the broth to boil. Check to see if the octopus is tender by probing with the tip of a paring knife. Remove the octopus from the broth and let cool to room temperature. (Reserve the savory broth to use in fish soup or Black Paella with Squid and Shrimp, page 239.)

When the octopus is cool, separate the tentacles with a sharp knife. Rub the tentacles with your fingers to remove any loose skin, then cut the tentacles into ¾-inch chunks. Keep at cool room temperature until ready to serve, or refrigerate for up to several hours, or overnight.

To serve, pile the octopus chunks onto a platter. Sprinkle with salt and pepper and drizzle with olive oil. Dust lightly with pimentón. Surround with the pickled onions. Supply diners with toothpicks or small skewers for communal snacking.

pickled onions

Slice 1 red onion into thin rings. Boil the onion slices in salted water for 1 minute. Drain and put the onion slices on a plate. Sprinkle with red wine vinegar. Let cool.

Potato and Salt Cod Tortilla

Potato, egg, and onion make tortilla española, a delicious, thick frittatalike cake that's a Spanish classic. The best tortillas are homemade—restaurant versions tend to be pretty rubbery. Sometimes other ingredients like chorizo or greens are added. For this all-fish menu, I added shredded salt cod, but it is optional. Two cups of olive oil may seem like a lot, but it serves as a poaching liquid and can be saved and used again to make more tortillas or to cook vegetables.

The tortilla can be prepared several hours ahead of time and held at room temperature. For the best texture and flavor, do not refrigerate or reheat it.

4 large russet potatoes
2 medium onions
2 cups olive oil
Salt and pepper

8 medium eggs
1 pound dried salt cod, softened
   (see Note) (optional)

Peel the potatoes and slice into ⅛-inch rounds. Slice the onions about the same thickness. Heat the olive oil in a large skillet and gently simmer the potatoes and onions, without letting them brown. When the potatoes and onions are soft—about 10 minutes—carefully drain them in a colander, reserving the olive oil.

Spread out the potatoes and onions on a baking sheet, season with salt and pepper, and cool to room temperature.

Beat the eggs in a large bowl. Add the shredded cod, if using, and the cooled potato-onion mixture. Stir gently to incorporate.

Heat 2 tablespoons of the reserved olive oil in a large cast-iron skillet over medium heat. Pour in the egg mixture and cook gently for 5 minutes, tilting the pan now and then to help the eggs set. Put a dinner plate over the top and carefully invert the tortilla onto the plate.

Add a little more oil to the pan, then slip the tortilla back into the pan to cook for 5 minutes on the other side. Flip the tortilla once more and cook for a few more minutes. Insert a small knife into the center of the tortilla to check for doneness—the knife should emerge clean. Put the tortilla on a serving platter and cool to room temperature.

To serve, cut the tortilla into small wedges or squares.

{NOTE ON} SOFTENING SALT COD

Shred the salt cod with your fingers. Rinse it well in a colander, then soak the cod in a large bowl of cold water for 4 to 6 hours (or overnight) to desalinate and soften it. Drain the fish and pat dry.

Sea Scallops a la Plancha

One of the delights of the winter season is the availability of good shellfish, especially sea scallops. Ask your fishmonger for freshly shucked scallops, often called "diver" scallops. A good way to cook them is *a la plancha,* on a hot griddle or cast-iron pan, which caramelizes the exterior and keeps them juicy inside.

1 pound large sea scallops, about 16
Salt and pepper
Olive oil

Green Sauce (recipe follows)
Lime wedges

Remove the "feet"—the tough muscle that attaches scallops to their shell—and discard (or add them to a fish stock). Season the scallops on both sides with salt and pepper and drizzle lightly with olive oil.

Heat a large griddle or cast-iron skillet to nearly smoking. Add the scallops in one layer, being careful not to crowd them. Brown the scallops well, letting them cook for 2 to 3 minutes. Turn the scallops over and cook for another 2 minutes.

Put the scallops on a platter and spoon a little green sauce onto each one. Surround with lime wedges.

green sauce

Put 1 small bunch cilantro, leaves and tender stems roughly chopped, 2 chopped garlic cloves, 1 sliced serrano chile, and 1 teaspoon cumin seeds, toasted and ground, in a blender. Season lightly with salt and add ½ cup olive oil. Blend to a smooth puree. Makes about 1 cup.

A SPANISH BREAKFAST

We've been drinking and dancing all night in a small village near Seville, eating radishes and olives and garbanzo soup in a dirt-floored bodega. As the sun is rising and most of the others depart, we're exhausted, but we want to keep the party going just a little longer. So we go over to Florita's tiny one-room apartment. Florita, as it turns out, is formerly Judy from Brooklyn, but she's been in Seville so long she looks and speaks like a gypsy.

Florita makes us strong coffee, then brings out a shallow earthenware platter, pours in an inch or so of Spanish olive oil, and a small handful of finely chopped garlic, coarse salt, and pepper. We drag chunks of crusty bread through the oil and eagerly wolf them down. Florita pours little glasses of a fiery liqueur. La Fernanda, a local flamenco star well into her sixties, lifts her tight skirt and does a little dance on the table. A few more jokes, a bit of a song, and we're out the door, everyone in dark glasses. Home to sleep the day away.

Black Paella with Squid and Shrimp

This is a simple paella with a deep, satisfying flavor. Squid ink (cuttlefish ink) turns the rice black and lends it sweetness. You can purchase packets of squid ink from a good fishmonger or Japanese grocery. I like to make this dish in the fireplace, but here's the stovetop method. A dab of garlic mayonnaise is traditional; you can use the Aïoli on page 102.

3 tablespoons olive oil

1 pound shrimp in the shell

Salt and pepper

1 large onion, finely diced

1 pound cleaned squid, bodies cut
   into thin rings and tentacles
   coarsely chopped

A pinch of crumbled saffron

¼ teaspoon cayenne

½ cup tomato puree

4 garlic cloves, smashed to a paste
   with a little salt

1 package squid ink, about 1 tablespoon

3 cups Bomba or Arborio rice

6 cups octopus broth (from Octopus
   Salad with Pickled Onions and
   Pimentón, page 229), Light Chicken
   Stock (page 73), or water

Preheat the oven to 350°F. Heat the olive oil in a 12-inch earthenware cazuela or paella pan over a medium flame. Add the shrimp, season with salt and pepper, and sauté briefly, just until the shrimp turn pink, about 1 to 2 minutes. Remove the shrimp and set aside.

Add the onion to the pan and let it sizzle in the oil. Cook for about 5 minutes, to brown a bit. Add the squid, season with salt and pepper, and cook for about 2 minutes more. Add the saffron, cayenne, tomato, garlic, squid ink, and rice, stirring well to coat the rice. Finally, add a large pinch of salt and the broth. Let the broth come to a full simmer. Taste the broth and adjust the seasoning. Simmer for 5 minutes.

Arrange the shrimp on top, then put the cazuela in the oven. Bake, uncovered, for 20 minutes. Remove and cover the pan with a clean dish towel. Let the paella rest for at least 15 minutes before serving. It tastes best just slightly warm.

serves 8–10

Membrillo and Sheep's-Milk Cheese

Membrillo is a firm jelly made of quinces. In Spain, it is highly appreciated for its affinity to cheese, especially Manchego, one of the most famous sheep's-milk cheeses. Though it is possible to make your own membrillo, I don't give a recipe here because so much good artisanal membrillo is now available in good cheese shops or specialty shops. French quince paste (*pâte de coing*) can be substituted, or try the fruit pastes from Mexico, called *ate,* made from guava, mango, or cactus fruit.

Membrillo can be sliced and served with thin slices of cheese on a plate. I also like to serve a large wedge of membrillo surrounded by an assortment of sheep's-milk cheeses, both Spanish and Italian, or firm goat cheeses or fresh mozzarella.

slow beef

Watercress, Beet, and Egg Salad

Braised Beef with Celery Root Mashed Potatoes

Roasted Apples

In praise of the braise: I was raised on brisket. The aroma of onions, bay, and beef broth—a sense memory that spans generations—filled my mother's house on a weekly basis. And I suppose that explains why, to me, rare grilled beef is awfully good, but braised or boiled beef is always better. I'm so surprised when people say they don't like stew. Stew employs the best of what cooking can do, and it can elevate the so-called lesser cuts to something glorious. After the initial and essential browning caramelizes the juices, the process of a long-simmered braise creates a succulent, complex sauce. Refrigerating the stew overnight only enhances those flavors. It's just so much more interesting than steak.

I find boiled beef irresistible. A Chez Panisse cook returning from an apprenticeship in a French kitchen revived for us the cook's treat: He'd retrieve a tender morsel of beef from the stockpot, then set out little dishes of coarse salt, little cornichons, and sharp mustard. We'd stand around the chopping block and snack on this simplest version of pot-au-feu.

Boiled meat has lots of guises. Many cultures derive secondary dishes from a weekly braise. Leftover Italian bollito misto can become a ravioli filling. A pot-au-feu can turn into boeuf à la vinaigrette the next day.

For a good beef braise, choose well-marbled stewing beef—bone-in cuts from the chuck, or front quarter of the cow, which will become tender from slow cooking. Flanken, cross-cut short ribs, make a particularly good braise, as do English-style short ribs, or thick-cut shoulder or chuck steaks. Meaty neck bones, oxtail, and beef cheeks can be prepared the same way, they just require a longer cooking time.

By the way, French custom dictates a good red wine with a roast, but an outstanding one with a stew.

Watercress, Beet, and Egg Salad

Look for watercress that is dark green, shiny, and utterly alive. If you can't find good watercress, substitute curly endive or a combination of baby spinach, arugula, upland cress, and Belgian endive.

3 bunches watercress

2 large shallots, finely diced

2 tablespoons red wine vinegar

1 tablespoon sherry vinegar

Salt and pepper

1 tablespoon Dijon mustard

¾ cup extra virgin olive oil

2 teaspoons grated orange zest

6 medium beets roasted (see Note), peeled, and diced small

6 Soft-Center Hard-Cooked Eggs (page 154)

Watercress is a little tricky to wash. If the leaves are cut from the stems before washing, they become jumbled and ratty. It is best to leave the bunch of watercress intact, wrapped in its rubber band. Swish the cress vigorously in a basin of cold water, then drain it, still tied, upside down in a colander. Shake the cress over the sink, wrap in a kitchen towel, and refrigerate.

To make the vinaigrette, macerate the diced shallots in a bowl with the vinegars and a good pinch of salt for 10 minutes. Stir in the mustard until dissolved. Whisk in the olive oil, add the orange zest, and grind in some pepper. Taste and adjust for acid and salt. The dressing should be somewhat tart so add more red wine vinegar if necessary.

Put the diced beets in a bowl and season them with salt and pepper. Whisk the vinaigrette and pour it over the beets. Toss the beets in the dressing and leave at room temperature.

To assemble the salad, trim short watercress sprigs from the bunch and make a fluffy pile on a large platter. Scatter the beets over the watercress leaves, distributing the vinaigrette here and there. Carefully cut the eggs into quarters and garnish the salad with them. Just before serving, sprinkle the eggs with salt and pepper. *serves 8–10*

{NOTE ON} ROASTED BEETS

Wash the beets, then put them, unpeeled, in a roasting pan with about an inch of water. Bake, covered, at 350°F for an hour, or until they are easily pierced with a fork. Slip off the skins while the beets are still warm. Roasted beets will keep for 2 or 3 days in the refrigerator.

Braised Beef with Celery Root Mashed Potatoes

The goal with a dish like this is tender, succulent meat and a concentrated, well-tempered sauce. Every braise benefits from a night in the refrigerator, so try to make this a day ahead. The only accompaniment I suggest is a potato puree flavored with celery root, which lends a curious perfumed counterpoint.

7 to 8 pounds flanken or
   2 large chuck steaks
Salt and pepper
Olive oil and vegetable oil or lard
2 tablespoons butter
2 tablespoons all-purpose flour
1 teaspoon paprika
½ cup tomato puree

1 cup dry red wine
8 cups Dark Chicken Stock (page 26)
2 large onions, halved
2 bay leaves
A few cloves
1 large thyme sprig
Celery Root Mashed Potatoes
   (recipe follows)

Season the beef generously with salt and pepper. Refrigerate for several hours, or overnight.

Preheat the oven to 325°F. Let the meat come to room temperature and dry it well.

For a good beef braise, it is essential to brown the meat well. Choose a cast-iron Dutch oven or heavy enameled iron pot. In ½ inch fat of your choice—a combination of olive and vegetable oil or lard—brown the beef (in batches if necessary) very well over medium-high heat. When the meat is well colored, about 8 minutes per side, remove it from the pot and set aside.

Pour off any fat left in the pot and return the pot to the flame. Add the butter and flour, stirring well with a wooden spoon to incorporate the flour. Stir in the paprika, tomato, and red wine, then slowly add the chicken stock and bring to a boil.

Add the onion halves, bay leaves, cloves, and thyme. Return the beef to the pot, cover, and transfer to the oven. Cook for about 2½ hours, or until the meat is quite tender.

Remove the braise from the oven and transfer the meat to a platter. Strain the sauce, then chill and degrease it. Taste the sauce and reseason if necessary. Put the beef back in the pot and pour the sauce back over it. If time allows, refrigerate overnight.

To serve, reheat the meat in its sauce. Remove the meat to a carving board and cut into thick slices. If necessary, reduce the sauce over a brisk flame to thicken it slightly.

Give each diner a piece of flanken with a good spoonful of sauce, along with a big spoonful of the celery root mashed potatoes. *serves 8–10*

celery root mashed potatoes

Mashed potatoes have become a medium for any number of trendy ingredients, but this pairing is classic and mutually beneficial: celery root sweetens the potatoes, while the potatoes render the celery root creamier.

1 celery root, about 1 pound

5 pounds Yukon Gold or other medium starchy potatoes

Salt and pepper

½ cup Crème Fraîche (page 41)

2 cups whole milk, warmed

½ pound (2 sticks) butter in chunks, at room temperature

Chives

Peel the celery root and cut into ½-inch slices. Peel the potatoes and cut into 2-inch chunks. Put both in a large heavy-bottomed pot and cover with cold water. The celery root and potatoes can stand at room temperature until ready to cook; start cooking about an hour before serving.

Add salt to the water, bring to a boil, and boil the vegetables briskly for 15 to 20 minutes, until the celery root is soft and the potatoes break easily when probed with a knife. Pour off 2 cups of the cooking water and reserve, then drain the vegetables in a large colander.

Return the vegetables to the pot, and mash them with a hand masher (or put them through a food mill or ricer for a smoother texture). Beat in the crème fraîche, milk, and butter. Season with salt and pepper.

Put the pot over medium heat, to heat the mash, beating occasionally. Thin with a little cooking water if necessary.

Serve in a large warmed bowl. Scatter finely minced chives over the top.

Roasted Apples

This simplest version of a baked apple, barely sugared and perfumed with a little Cognac, yields concentrated, caramelized juices. Look for local baking apples at your farmers' market. Make sure they are all of the same size.

8 baking apples   Cognac
Sugar

Preheat the oven to 375°F. Employing a twisting motion with a paring knife, remove the stem from each apple in a conical shape. Reserve the stems. Carefully scoop out the apple cores with a melon baller or small sturdy spoon, leaving ½ inch or so of flesh at the bottom of the apples.

Put the apples in an earthenware baking dish. Fill each apple with sugar, then add a splash of Cognac to each one. Replace the stems and sprinkle sugar generously over the tops.

Bake the apples on the top shelf of the oven for 45 minutes to an hour, until the skins burst. Serve at room temperature, making sure to spoon the juices over each portion.

nuevo mexico

Avocado Quesadillas

Spicy Pickled Vegetables

Green Chile Stew

Bizcochitos

All cooks have their culinary eccentricities. It's said that the French painter Toulouse-Lautrec always carried a nutmeg grater in his pocket—you never know. My version of culinary insurance, for perking up the bland, is to always travel with a handful of fresh chiles in my pocket. I developed a craving for cooking with chiles while living in New Mexico; ever since, I carry them with me, to be sure.

Cooking in New Mexico, I learned about *caribe,* which are nothing more than semihot dried red chile crushed coarsely and used as a table condiment or added to cooked dishes. Now I use *caribe* freely.

New Mexican cuisine, with its base of austere Spanish peasant fare, influenced by Mexican and Native American cultures, is anything but subtle. Chiles, both red and green, fresh and dried, are the crucial ingredient. In the harsh high-desert climate, chile plants somehow survive drought, hail, and summer monsoons, just as the early settlers did, and their flavor is all the better for their suffering.

A few native chile varieties are still grown on small family farms in the north. In microclimates such as the one around Chimayo, sandy soil produces extraordinarily flavorful chiles: chiles with *terroir*. Farther south, around Hatch, dependable hybrid chiles are grown on a large scale, descendants of the New Mexico Number Nine, a cousin of the California Anaheim—though New Mexico green chiles are usually hotter.

The chile harvest is in the fall. People buy big bags of them and line up to have them roasted by entrepreneurial chile roasters who set up in supermarket parking lots or at roadside stands. The chiles must be roasted to remove their tough skins. I love this annual ritual that fills the air with the sweet scent of charred peppers.

In the old days, green chiles were eaten as a seasonal autumn treat or canned for winter. These days most people pack their roasted green chiles in small zipper bags and load them in the freezer, thawing a bag or two as needed.

Avocado Quesadillas

This simple but surprisingly tasty quesadilla is easy to make at the last minute, then cut into wedges to serve with drinks. Try to look for avocados that are ripe but still firm. A little chopped epazote—a rather pungent Mexican herb, found in Latino groceries (or easily grown)—adds an authentic flavor to the Onion Relish and the Spicy Pickled Vegetables. In Mexico, epazote is traditionally used for cooking beans as well.

Large flour tortillas
Fresh mozzarella or queso oaxaqueño,
   thinly sliced
Avocados, pitted, peeled,
   and thinly sliced

Salt and pepper
Onion Relish (recipe follows)
Green Cilantro and Tomatillo Salsa
   (page 141)

Preheat a cast-iron griddle, comal, or frying pan over a medium flame. Adjust the heat as necessary to keep the pan hot. Lay a tortilla on the griddle, then quickly layer it with thin slices of mozzarella and avocado. Sprinkle with salt and pepper, then spoon on some onion relish. Lay another tortilla over the top.

After about a minute, flip the quesadilla and toast the other side. Both sides should be mottled and crisp, and the cheese should be beginning to ooze. Remove the quesadilla to a cutting board, cut into wedges, and serve with the salsa.

Keep the griddle hot, and continue to make more quesadillas as necessary.

onion relish

Take a couple of sweet onions, cut them into fine dice, and put them in a bowl. Add some finely minced jalapeño or serrano chile, a handful of finely chopped cilantro, a few leaves of epazote, finely chopped, and salt and pepper. Mix well and squeeze some lime juice over the relish. Taste for seasoning, then refrigerate until needed.

Spicy Pickled Vegetables

These pickles will keep for a week or two, refrigerated, but they taste best at room temperature. They're good with drinks, as an accompaniment to Avocado Quesadillas, or served with stewed or roasted meats or cold cuts.

4 large carrots, peeled and sliced into
    ½-inch-thick rounds
2 medium onions, sliced into thick
    half-moons
3 or 4 jalapeño chiles, quartered
    lengthwise
4 garlic cloves, peeled
1 teaspoon salt, or to taste

10 peppercorns
1 teaspoon coriander seeds
A small epazote sprig (optional)
1 bay leaf
1 tablespoon cider vinegar
1 tablespoon olive oil
1 teaspoon dried Mexican oregano

Put the carrots, onions, jalapeños, garlic, salt, peppercorns, coriander seeds, epazote, bay leaf, vinegar, and olive oil in a large saucepan and cover with water. Bring to a boil, then reduce to a simmer and cook until the carrots are just cooked through. Transfer to a bowl to cool.

When the vegetables are cool, add the oregano. Taste and add salt if necessary.

Green Chile Stew

In northern New Mexico, green chile stew is legendary. Everybody makes it, everybody eats it, and everybody loves it, even if everybody makes a different version—with or without potatoes, or tomatoes, or cumin, or tomatillos, or cilantro, but never without a healthy amount of green chile. Pork stew is the favorite, but it can be made with lamb, beef, chicken, or turkey too. Green chile stew is good any time of year, but it is especially welcome on a cold winter night. It makes a great burrito with rice and beans, but I like it best in a bowl, with warm, thick corn tortillas on the side.

5 pounds well-marbled boneless pork
   butt, cut into 2-inch cubes

Salt and pepper

2 tablespoons vegetable oil or lard

2 large onions, finely diced

4 to 6 garlic cloves, chopped

2 teaspoons cumin seeds,
   toasted and finely ground

½ cup chopped tomatoes,
   fresh or canned

6 large carrots, peeled and chunked

1 cup chopped roasted green chiles
   (see Note), or more as you like

2 tablespoons all-purpose flour

8 cups water or chicken broth

3 pounds russet potatoes,
   peeled and cut into large dice

Chopped cilantro

Hot corn or flour tortillas

Season the meat with salt and pepper. Heat the oil or lard in a large Dutch oven or other heavy-bottomed pot. Add the meat, in several batches, without crowding, and brown it lightly. Transfer to a platter or tray.

Add the onions to the pot and brown them. Add the garlic, cumin, tomatoes, carrots, and green chiles, then sprinkle the flour over and stir. Salt the mixture, then return the browned meat to the pot and stir well. Cover with the water or broth and bring to a boil.

Cover the pot, turn the flame to low, and simmer gently for 1 hour.

Taste the broth and fiddle with it, adding salt or more green chile as necessary. The broth should be well seasoned and fairly spicy. Add the potatoes and continue cooking for 30 minutes, or until the potatoes are soft and the meat is quite tender. Skim any fat from the surface of the broth.

Let the stew rest for an hour or more. Refrigerate overnight if desired.

To serve, reheat the stew and ladle into warmed bowls. Sprinkle with chopped cilantro and accompany with hot tortillas.   *serves 8–10*

{NOTE ON} ROASTING GREEN CHILES

Fresh green chiles, such as New Mexico or Anaheim, must be roasted over an open flame on a barbecue grill, gas burner, or under the broiler, till blackened. Then rub off the skins, remove the stems and seeds, and coarsely chop the chiles. Twelve large fresh chiles will yield approximately 1 cup of chopped. Lacking these, a pretty fair approximation can be made with a combination of roasted fresh poblano chiles (sometimes called pasillas) and roasted jalapeños. Frozen green chiles are an acceptable substitute for fresh; use commercially canned chiles only as a last resort.

Bizcochitos

These anise-flavored sugar cookies, made with lard, are another traditional New Mexican specialty. Don't be tempted to make them with butter—they won't have their characteristic flakiness. Be forewarned: they are addictive.

1 cup sugar

1 cup good-quality lard or organic
   vegetable shortening

1 large egg

½ teaspoon vanilla extract

¼ cup brandy or sherry

2 teaspoons anise seeds

3 cups all-purpose flour

1 teaspoon baking powder

½ teaspoon salt

2 teaspoons cinnamon, mixed
   with ¾ cup sugar

With an electric mixer, cream the sugar and lard well in a large bowl. Beat in the egg, vanilla extract, and brandy. Add the anise seeds. Sift together the flour, baking powder, and salt. Mix the flour mixture into the lard mixture and knead for a few minutes (by machine or by hand). Add a little water if necessary to make a soft dough.

Divide the dough in half. Roll the dough into logs about 2 inches in diameter. Wrap each log in plastic and refrigerate till firm.

Preheat the oven to 350°F. Slice the dough into ¼-inch rounds and place the rounds on parchment-lined baking sheets. Sprinkle each cookie lightly with the cinnamon-sugar mixture. Bake for 12 minutes or so, until golden. Cool on a rack.

makes about 5 dozen cookies

feeling italian, part III

Orecchiette al Forno

Lamb Osso Buco with Orange, Lemon, and Capers

Persimmon Pudding

I had a stylish great aunt who considered herself worldly and a discerning gourmet (she had eaten steak Diane on numerous occasions). Having lived in Cleveland, she gloried in an elegance many women in our town of Dayton lacked. Her perfectly coiffed silver hair was swept back in a flip, and she wore that hairdo forever. The hair, the handbag, the heels, the string of pearls, and always, the cape. Great Aunt Sally was a woman who could wear a cape.

She wasn't Italian, but she advised me as a boy never to cook more than one pound of pasta at a time. I figured this was an idea she'd read somewhere or had on the word of some Italian chef on a cruise.

Aunt Sally had gained some notoriety for her spaghetti soirées, to which she'd invite masses of people. Everyone had to wait their turn as she held sway, cooking just one box of pasta at a time. She took the lesson to the extreme: since she only had one pot, she could feed only four people at a time. Of course, she could have bought another pot and served eight. But she just had the one pot.

In any case, I promised her I'd never cook more than a pound of pasta at a time. And I never do. Aunt Sally got it half-right: it's never a good idea to cook more

than one pound of pasta at a time, for pasta needs lots of water. But I take a different approach to cooking pasta for a group. For four or fewer, I'll cook it to order, one pound at a time. Or, for a few more people, I'll use two pots—still only a pound in each pot. Actually, for a bigger group, I'll make pasta *al forno,* a baked pasta, cooking the pasta ahead and saucing it, then sliding the dish into the oven just before serving to cook until it's bubbly.

It's funny. Though Aunt Sally gave me a cooking lesson I never forgot, I cannot remember her ever cooking for me.

Orecchiette al Forno

If you choose a sturdy dried pasta type like *orecchiette* (little ears), you can cook pasta ahead without compromising quality. For a vegetarian version of this baked pasta, omit the sausage and add crushed fennel seeds to the greens. Other greens can be easily substituted for the rapini, if you like.

2 pounds orecchiette	2 teaspoons finely chopped rosemary
Olive oil	Red pepper flakes
2 pounds rapini (broccoli rabe), washed	Salt
1 pound Fennel Sausage	½ pound fresh ricotta
(recipe follows)	Butter
4 garlic cloves, chopped	Grated pecorino

Have two pots of well-salted water boiling briskly. Cook 1 pound of pasta in each pot until extremely al dente, about 9 minutes. Lift the pasta from the water and spread on baking sheets to cool; drizzle lightly with olive oil to keep it from sticking together.

Using the boiling water, blanch the greens for 1 minute or so. Drain in a colander. When they are cool, roughly chop the greens and set aside.

In a large skillet, lightly brown the sausage meat, breaking it up with a wooden spoon as it cooks so it crumbles into small pieces. Remove the browned sausage from the pan.

Pour off any fat from the pan and return the pan to the stove. Add 2 tablespoons olive oil and heat over medium heat. Warm the garlic in the oil, but don't let it brown. Add the chopped greens, rosemary, and a little red pepper. Lightly salt the greens, stir them around the pan, and turn off the heat.

To assemble the dish, put the cooked pasta, cooked greens, and cooked sausage in a large bowl and mix gently. Add the ricotta and mix again.

Butter two shallow earthenware gratin dishes. Put half the pasta mixture in each dish. Sprinkle lightly with grated pecorino. Cover and keep at room temperature for up to several hours.

Preheat the oven to 400°F. Shortly before serving time, bake the pasta for 15 minutes. Uncover and bake for 5 minutes more.

Serve the pasta in warmed soup plates. Pass grated pecorino at the table.

fennel sausage

Much commercially made sausage is of dubious origin, filled with preservatives and odd synthetic seasonings. It's very easy to make fennel sausage at home. This recipe yields double the amount of sausage needed for the orecchiette. Of course you could halve it, but I suggest you make the whole recipe—just wrap the remainder well and freeze.

2 pounds ground pork shoulder,
  not too lean

2 teaspoons salt

2 teaspoons crushed fennel seed

1 teaspoon red pepper flakes

4 garlic cloves, finely chopped

Working quickly, to keep the meat quite cold, mix all the ingredients well. Refrigerate immediately and use within 2 days, or freeze in small packages for later use.

Lamb Osso Buco with Orange, Lemon, and Capers

This osso buco is made with lamb instead of the traditional veal shanks. Whole lamb shanks always look gargantuan to me, so I have the butcher cut each shank into three pieces.

I use a technique for cooking them that is not traditional: After seasoning the meat, I simmer it for an hour with aromatics, which provides a light broth from which to make a sauce. Then I finish the shanks by baking them in the sauce.

As with most stews, making the dish the day before both eases preparation and improves flavor. Osso buco is customarily served sprinkled with gremolata, a mixture of parsley, lemon zest, and garlic. Here I add orange zest and capers. I often serve steamed potatoes or polenta with the shanks.

10 lamb shanks, cut crosswise in thirds
  (have the butcher do this)

Salt and pepper

2 large onions

1 large carrot, peeled and chunked

1 celery stalk, coarsely chopped

2 bay leaves

1 thyme sprig

A few cloves

3 tablespoons butter

3 tablespoons all-purpose flour

2 tablespoons tomato paste

1 tablespoon powdered dried porcini
  (optional)

2 cups dry white wine

Gremolata (recipe follows)

Trim the excess fat from the lamb shanks and season them generously with salt and pepper. Put the shanks in a large heavy-bottomed pot and cover with cold water. Add the onions, carrot, celery, bay leaves, thyme, and cloves. Bring the water to a boil, skimming any surfacing foam, then turn the flame to low.

Cover the pot and simmer the meat until cooked through but still firm, about 1 hour. Remove the meat, then strain and reserve the broth.

In a large saucepan, melt the butter over medium heat. Stir in the flour and brown carefully, stirring, until just past golden. Add the tomato paste and porcini powder, if using. Slowly whisk in 10 cups of the reserved lamb broth, 1 cup at a time, allowing the sauce to thicken after each addition.

Simmer the sauce gently for 15 minutes. Taste and adjust the seasoning. The finished sauce will be only barely thickened but will have good color and body.

Preheat the oven to 375°F. Put the cooked lamb shanks in two low earthenware dishes, in one layer, with the bones sticking up. Mix the wine into the sauce and pour the sauce over the shanks to come halfway up each dish.

Bake the lamb shanks, uncovered, until the tops are well browned, about 20 minutes. Now cover the shanks, reduce the heat to 350°F, and bake for another 40 minutes or so, until the meat is quite tender. At this point you can serve the shanks hot from the oven, if desired.

Uncover the lamb and cool in its sauce to room temperature. Refrigerate overnight if desired.

To reheat, bring the dish to room temperature and bake, covered, at 400°F for 15 to 20 minutes.

Serve the lamb shanks steaming hot directly from the baking dishes. Sprinkle the gremolata liberally over the entire dishes just before bringing them to the table. Serve each diner 3 meaty bones with a good spoonful of sauce.

serves 8–10

gremolata

Don't make the gremolata too far in advance, or the fresh flavors will diminish and the garlic will get too strong tasting. It can, however, be made up to an hour ahead and refrigerated.

Chop only the leaves of 1 large bunch flat-leaf parsley—not too fine—and put it in a bowl. Remove the zest from 1 orange and 1 lemon with a vegetable peeler or zester. Finely mince the zest. Mash 2 garlic cloves to a fine paste with a little salt. Chop 2 tablespoons capers. Cut a few scallions into fine slivers or chop fine. Add the zest, garlic, capers, and scallions to the chopped parsley and mix well.

Persimmon Pudding

This recipe comes from a cook from the South, named (yes) Mrs. West, who regularly collects wild persimmons to make it. Ripe Hachiya or Fuyu persimmons from the market will work well. If using Hachiyas, they must be very ripe. This pudding is a bit more like a flan than a cake, and will keep well, refrigerated, for a few days.

Persimmon pudding reminds me of Italy in winter, when you encounter the bright orange fruits hanging from their bare branches. The pudding will puff up while it bakes, then flatten.

2 cups chopped persimmon flesh
    (from 4–5 large persimmons)
¾ cup sugar
1 cup buttermilk
2 large eggs, beaten
1½ cups all-purpose flour
2 teaspoons baking powder

1 cup half-and-half
1 teaspoon baking soda
⅓ cup butter
½ teaspoon cinnamon
1 teaspoon vanilla extract
Barely Whipped Cream (page 69)

Preheat the oven to 325°F. Puree the persimmons with the sugar and ½ cup buttermilk in a food processor. Use a fine meshed strainer to strain into a large bowl. Beat in the eggs.

Sift the flour with the baking powder. Combine the half-and-half with the rest of the buttermilk and the baking soda. Add the flour mixture to the persimmon and eggs alternately with the buttermilk mixture, stirring well after each addition.

Melt the butter. Paint a 9-by-13-inch baking pan with some of the butter, and pour the remainder into the batter. Add the cinnamon and vanilla and beat well, then pour the batter into the pan.

Bake for 1 hour, or until a knife inserted in the center comes out clean. Cool the pudding on a rack.

To serve, cut into squares and accompany with the whipped cream.

peasant fare from a parisian kitchen

Pig's Ear Salad with Herb Vinaigrette

Duck Hams with French Lentils and Celery Root Rémoulade

Chilled Prunes in Beaujolais

I picked up and moved to Paris on a whim. I was there on holiday in the spring of 2001 and found myself at dinner with some ex-pats at my friend Peggy's place on the rue Madame. One of them was about to give up his apartment; did I want to come by to look at it? I'd heard about the place, in a seventeenth-century building in the Latin Quarter. The next day, I stopped by and, within minutes, I decided to take it.

I couldn't move immediately—I had to return to San Francisco and give notice at Chez Panisse. I was the chef in the downstairs restaurant and I'd been there on and off for almost twenty-five years. Alice knew I had been wondering what to do next. She was stoic but gracious when I told her I would be leaving in six months.

I was more than ready to leave the grueling, stressful work of a restaurant kitchen. Aiming for perfection every night takes a toll, physically and mentally. A year away from the restaurant seemed a necessary tonic. I sublet our San Francisco apartment, and just days after 9/11, headed off to France with my companion, Randal, and our two dogs.

Why Paris? Actually, I wondered that myself. Was I such an incurable

Francophile that I had always dreamed of living there? Was French food to me the pinnacle of pinnacles? Not really. There were lots of other places where I could imagine spending a year, and certainly many other cuisines I'm drawn to. But I'd visited Paris often, so it made sense to me. My high-school French was good enough to get by. I liked the daily routines of Parisian life; the markets were a real draw. Paris for me was an easy leap into Europe, close to some of the more exotic places of my fantasies.

But, above all, Paris was a place for cooks. (I may have been tired of restaurant work, but I certainly didn't intend to stop cooking—it's the *cooking* part that I like.) The streets are literally teeming with foodstuffs, and while it may not be as easy to get a good meal as in the past, the tradition of serious attention to food prevails.

With enough time and the markets so full of good food, I began to cook. But I had to learn to work with serious limitations: a closet-sized kitchen, only two gas burners, a vintage electric oven, a little sink, and a rigged-up work counter. Well, and the fireplace in the living room for grilling. Aside from figuring out how to work in a tiny kitchen, I had to learn how to use it to prepare a meal for a crowd. From the start, we were doing dinners for twelve people, because my inclination is always the more the merrier, and our friends always had friends. The meals had to be flavorful yet easy to execute. Everything would come to the table in large platters. In fact, it was in that Parisian kitchen that the idea for this book was born.

We'd been to a couple of dinner salons in Paris and we thought we could do it so much better. With me in the kitchen and Randal as an experienced maitre d' to literally handle the front of the house, we decided to start a dinner club. We named it Aux Chiens Lunatiques, after those old bistros like Au Chat Qui Fume, and our two dogs.

We'd invite friends and strangers, and pass a jar for contributions. Word of mouth spread the news. We'd have three courses and wonderful cheeses. We'd serve a simple paella cooked in the fireplace, or a whole lamb shoulder braised for hours with Moroccan spices, or a lavish New Year's fête. It was a hit from the start. In fact, the menu that follows came from a Beaujolais Nouveau dinner Aux Chiens.

Pig's Ear Salad with Herb Vinaigrette

In Paris, this dish would seem like old-fashioned bistro fare, yet any discerning Frenchman would appreciate it as easily as haute cuisine. Of course, you could substitute a platter of charcuterie, but I encourage you to be adventuresome and experience the true pleasure of sliced pig's ears dressed with a zippy vinaigrette. This recipe can be easily prepared over the course of two or three days. First the ears are salted, then simmered and sliced. That done, they'll keep for several days. The finished dish is assembled in just a few minutes.

Order pig's ears from your butcher, or find them easily in a Chinese or Latino market.

8 to 10 pig's ears, about 2 pounds, or a
   combination of ears and snouts
Salt and pepper
1 onion, sliced
2 garlic cloves
2 carrots, peeled and cut into chunks
1 bay leaf

1 thyme branch
2 cloves
A few peppercorns
Herb Vinaigrette (recipe follows)
1 large bunch radishes, trimmed,
   washed, and slivered

Layer the ears in a large stainless steel or glass bowl, heavily salting each layer. Leave them for a couple of hours at room temperature, or refrigerate overnight.

Rinse the ears and put in a large stockpot. Barely cover with water. Add the onion, garlic, carrots, bay leaf, thyme branch, cloves, and peppercorns. Bring to a simmer and simmer gently for about 2 hours or so, until the ears are tender (some cartilage will remain crunchy). Let the ears cool in the cooking liquid.

When the ears are cool, slice them into ¼-inch ribbons, discarding any tough bits, and put them in a wide bowl.

Strain the broth and pour enough broth over the ears just to cover. Cover the bowl and refrigerate.

When chilled, the pig's ear slices will be suspended in a firm jelly. The dish can be served right away or covered and kept for several days; its flavor will only improve.

To serve, invert the jellied pig's ears onto a platter and unmold. Spoon the vinaigrette over the top, then garnish with lots of slivered radishes and a sprinkling of salt and fresh pepper.

The pig's ear salad can be cut into rough wedges or scooped with a spoon.

herb vinaigrette

This dressing is also good with cooked vegetables, such as boiled leeks, steamed potatoes, or roasted beets, and with boiled ham or beef.

Finely dice a large shallot, put in a small bowl, and cover with 2 to 3 tablespoons red wine vinegar. Add a little salt and pepper. Macerate, then stir in 2 teaspoons of Dijon mustard. Add a cup of olive oil, 1 tablespoon chopped cornichons, 2 teaspoons chopped capers, a mixture of finely chopped thyme, tarragon, chervil, parsley, and some slivered scallions. Taste and adjust the seasoning, adding a little more vinegar if necessary.

Duck Hams with French Lentils and Celery Root Rémoulade

This is a method for brining duck so it tastes like ham, and the resulting duck ham can be used any way a regular ham can be—to make duck-ham scrambled eggs, for instance, or in white bean soup. The duck is brine-cured for a few days, to transform it. I prefer to use Pekin (Long Island) duck legs for this dish, as they tend to be more tender and juicy than the larger moulard or Muscovy legs.

I am completely enamored of these duck hams, which taste like both duck and ham, and are perfect with warm humble lentils. They have the same appeal as duck confit, but are more unusual, and even a little lighter.

12 duck legs, about 6 pounds

FOR THE BRINE

8 cups water

¼ cup salt

1 teaspoon peppercorns

3 or 4 allspice berries

2 bay leaves

1 large thyme sprig or 1 teaspoon
    dried thyme

A few cloves

1 scant teaspoon curing salt

FOR THE BROTH

1 onion

1 celery stalk

1 carrot, peeled

Several garlic cloves

A few thyme sprigs

1 bay leaf

2 or 3 cloves

A few peppercorns

French Lentils (page 274)

Celery Root Rémoulade (page 275)

To brine the duck, trim the legs of excess skin and fat. Reserve the trimmings for making rendered duck fat (see Note). Put the duck legs in a nonreactive container.

Whisk together the brine ingredients, and pour the brine over the duck legs. Make sure the meat is submerged in the brine. Refrigerate for 2 to 3 days, or up to a week.

To cook the duck, remove the legs from the brine and put them in a large pot. Cover generously with water and add the onion, celery, carrot, garlic, thyme branches, bay leaf, cloves, and peppercorns. Bring to a simmer, and simmer gently for about 40 minutes, until the meat yields easily to a skewer or paring knife. Remove the legs and set aside to cool. Strain and reserve the broth for the lentils.

To finish the dish, preheat the oven to 375°F. Divide the cooked lentils between two earthenware gratin dishes. Moisten each dish with 2 cups of the duck broth. Arrange 6 duck legs, skin side up, over the lentils in each dish.

Bake for 30 minutes, covered. Then bake for 15 minutes uncovered, or until the duck legs have browned a bit and the lentils are steaming hot.

Serve each diner a large spoonful of lentils and nestle a duck ham on top. Pass the celery root rémoulade separately, or put a small spoonful on each plate.

serves 12

{NOTE ON} RENDERING DUCK FAT

Place the trimmings in a small saucepan, add a cup of water, and simmer slowly for 30 to 40 minutes. Strain the fat and refrigerate. Duck fat can be kept for a month, and it is useful for making panfried potatoes (or chopped liver).

DUCK LEG TRIVIA

12 duck legs = 6 pounds
1 untrimmed duck leg = 8 to 9 ounces
1 trimmed duck leg = 7 to 8 ounces
Trimmings from 12 legs = 1 pound
Yield from 1 pound trimmings = 1½ cups rendered duck fat

french lentils

This is a wonderful way to make lentils, duck legs or no. Serve hot with the duck hams, or at room temperature for a lentil salad, adding a few drops of red wine vinegar and a splash of olive oil.

2 pounds (4 cups) small French green
    lentils (lentilles de Puy)
8 cups duck ham broth (see above),
    or Light Chicken Stock
    (page 73), or water
Salt and pepper

1 small bunch carrots, about ½ pound
2 medium onions
1 celery heart, about ½ pound
2 tablespoons duck fat or olive oil
Thyme sprigs
Sage leaves

Pick over and rinse the lentils. Put in a saucepan, cover with broth, add a little salt, and simmer until just done, about 20 minutes. Drain the cooked lentils.

Dice the carrots, onions, and celery and stew gently in the duck fat, adding salt, pepper, and a little chopped thyme and sage, until softened, about 10 minutes. Combine the stewed vegetables and lentils. Check the seasoning.

celery root rémoulade

Celery root is typically dressed with mayonnaise, but here it's bathed in crème fraîche, mustard, and horseradish. I like to serve this salad with the duck and lentils, as a sort of condiment. But it's also a lovely first course, paired with smoked fish and watercress.

1½ pounds celery root
Salt and pepper
Juice of 1 large lemon
½ cup Crème Fraîche (page 41)

¼ cup Dijon mustard
2 tablespoons grated horseradish
Cayenne (optional)
Chives

Peel the celery root and cut into matchstick shapes about 3 inches long. Put the celery root in a bowl. Salt lightly, then add the lemon juice and toss well. Cover tightly and refrigerate for at least an hour, or overnight.

Drain the celery root and blot with towels. Dress with the crème fraîche, mustard, and horseradish. Add salt and pepper to taste—a pinch of cayenne is good too. Sprinkle with finely slivered chives.

Chilled Prunes in Beaujolais

Prunes have been so maligned they are now marketed as "dried plums" by the California Dried Plum Board (which was formerly the California Prune Board). Plumped up by a simmer in young Beaujolais, prunes make a pleasing and refreshing dessert.

This is by far the best use I've found for Beaujolais Nouveau, that wine bottled one month or so after harvest as a novelty or, as some believe, a marketing ploy. I like the festive aspect of a Beaujolais Nouveau party, but I'd rather drink real wine with dinner and save the Nouveau for cooking—though I usually do take a curious sip or two.

1½ pounds pitted organic prunes

2½ cups Beaujolais Nouveau or other
   light-bodied red wine

½ cup sugar

Cinnamon stick

Combine all the ingredients in a saucepan and simmer for 10 minutes. Turn off the heat. Chill before serving (up to several days).

Serve each diner a small bowl with a few prunes floating in the winey sauce. The prunes are best served quite cold, chased with the red wine juice.

north african comfort food

Carrot and Coriander Salad

Chicken Tagine with Pumpkin and Chickpeas

Walnut Cigars

What a strange idea: "comfort food." Isn't every food comforting in its own way? Why are certain foods disqualified? Can't fancy food be soothing in the same way as granny food? Must it always be about loaded memories, like Proust's madeleine? Or can it be merely quirky, like M. F. K. Fisher's tangerine ritual: she dried them on a radiator, then cooled them on her Paris windowsill.

Comfort food—food that reassures—is different things to different people. For some, the phrase conjures meat loaf and mashed potatoes, or stuffed cabbage rolls, or just a good roast chicken. For a friend who's traveled quite a lot in Southeast Asia, Chinese rice porridge, the salty kind, replaced his mother's oatmeal as a kind of touchstone. For me, comfort is Champagne and oysters, *and* it's a chicken stew, perhaps dating back to a childhood hot lunch dish, made by a doting aunt who called it "chicken in sauce." I called it "goopy chicken," and I loved it.

I still have a fondness for any sort of chicken braise, from chicken and dumplings to Oaxacan chicken mole. Just about every culture cooks a chicken, as I discovered on my travels, so I was not surprised to find that a Moroccan chicken tagine produced a familiar soothing sensation—not unlike the chicken stew of my childhood.

Carrot and Coriander Salad

French cooks make a raw grated carrot salad they call *carottes rapées,* dressed with a sharp vinaigrette, to accompany cold meats. This spiced Moroccan version makes a fine first course. If you have a machine that produces a small julienne, now's the time to use it. Or, use a vegetable slicer (Benriner type) to cut the carrots into thin lengthwise slices, then julienne with a sharp knife. An ordinary box grater doesn't work well for this salad—it grates the carrots to too fine a pulp.

Surround the salad with Soft-Center Hard-Cooked Eggs (page 154), if you like.

2 pounds carrots, peeled

Salt and pepper

1 large shallot, finely diced

2 garlic cloves, smashed to a paste
    with a little salt

2 teaspoons cumin seeds,
    toasted and ground

2 teaspoons coriander seeds,
    toasted and ground

Red pepper flakes or cayenne

Juice of 1 or 2 lemons

Olive oil

Limes

Good green olives, such as Picholine
    or Lucques (not pitted)

1 bunch cilantro

Julienne the carrots into long slivers, put them in a large bowl, sprinkle lightly with salt, and toss. Add the shallot, garlic, cumin, coriander, red pepper, and lemon juice. Toss well, and let the carrots soften a bit.

Add olive oil to coat, then adjust the seasoning with lemon juice, salt, black pepper, and red pepper. Cover and set aside at cool room temperature for up to several hours, or refrigerate and then return to room temperature to serve.

Toss the salad again to distribute the seasoning, and heap on a large platter. Squeeze a little fresh lime juice over, and garnish with green olives. Roughly chop some cilantro and scatter it over the salad. I like to strew tender sprigs of cilantro and lime wedges around the salad (or, for a spicier version, slivered red onions and jalapeño chiles).

Chicken Tagine with Pumpkin and Chickpeas

Saffron-scented North African–style chicken tagine is a wonderful stew, perfect for a small group, comforting on a cold night. In Tunisia and Morocco, *tagine* is both the name of the cooking vessel and the dish. Basically, a deep thick earthenware plate is filled with meat and vegetables or dried fruit. A high conical lid keeps the moisture in, allowing the dish to simmer, sizzle, and bake, on a propane stovetop or over hot coals. The tagine is a clever device, economical in a land where the price of fuel is high and most homes do not have ovens. Similar results can be achieved in an American oven using a wide shallow casserole or gratin dish.

This tagine can be made hours (or a day) before serving, and then is easily reheated. The recipe is easy to alter for other seasons (it's wonderful with tomatoes in place of pumpkin).

FOR THE CHICKPEAS

1 pound (2 cups) dried chickpeas, picked over and soaked overnight in cold water

1 large onion, quartered

1 cinnamon stick

A few cloves

Olive oil

Salt

Butter

Pinch of ground cinnamon

Chopped parsley

FOR THE TAGINE

About 4 pounds pumpkin or winter squash, seeds and membranes removed

Salt and pepper

12 large whole chicken legs (with thighs)

A 3-inch piece of ginger, peeled and grated

2 teaspoons cumin seeds, lightly toasted and roughly ground

4 large onions, diced small

2 tablespoons olive oil

2 tablespoons butter

6 garlic cloves, sliced

Large pinch of saffron

Red pepper flakes or cayenne

Harissa Oil (recipe follows)

To cook the chickpeas, drain them, put in a saucepan, and cover with 3 quarts of water. Add the onion, cinnamon stick, cloves, a splash of olive oil, and a little salt. Bring to a boil, then simmer gently uncovered, for about an hour, or until the chickpeas are tender. Taste for salt and adjust. Leave the chickpeas to cool in the cooking liquid.

For the tagine, cut the pumpkin or winter squash into thick slices and spread them on a flat surface. Season the slices with salt and pepper.

Season the chicken legs generously with salt and pepper. Massage them with the grated ginger. Sprinkle the cumin seeds over the meat. Set the chicken aside.

Preheat the oven to 400°F. In a skillet over medium heat, sauté the diced onions in a combination of butter and olive oil until softened. Season with salt and continue cooking until the onions are lightly golden, about 10 minutes. Turn off the heat and add the sliced garlic cloves. Crumble the saffron over the onions. Stir the onions and season to taste with red pepper.

Arrange the onions in a shallow earthenware casserole (or two if necessary), then top with the pumpkin slices. Now put chicken legs over the pumpkin in one layer, skin side up. Add 3 to 4 cups of chickpea cooking liquid, barely covering the chicken.

Cover the casserole and bake for 20 minutes or so, until the liquid is bubbling briskly. Reduce the heat to 375°F and continue cooking for another 30 minutes, or until the chicken legs yield easily to a probing fork. Take the casserole from the oven and remove the chicken legs. Skim any surfacing fat with a shallow ladle.

Replace the chicken legs and return the dish to the oven, uncovered. Bake until the juices are bubbling and the chicken legs are lightly browned, about 20 minutes.

Warm the chickpeas in their cooking liquid, then drain and deposit them in a warmed bowl. Swirl in a little butter, the cinnamon, and some chopped parsley.

Serve each diner a chicken leg with some pumpkin and good ladle of broth. Spoon some chickpeas over each serving. Pass a bowl of the spicy harissa oil for drizzling.   *serves 8–10*

harissa oil

This is a fragrant, spicy, ruddy-colored oil, to be drizzled over any number of things—olives, eggs, vegetables, toasted bread, or chicken stew.

1 tablespoon cumin seeds

1 tablespoon coriander seeds

1 teaspoon caraway seeds

1 teaspoon fennel seeds

3 tablespoons sweet paprika or mild
   ground red chile

1 teaspoon cayenne or other powdered
   hot red chile

1 to 2 garlic cloves, smashed to a paste
   with a little salt

1 teaspoon salt

1 cup olive oil

A few drops of red wine vinegar

Toast all the seeds in a dry pan over medium heat until they are fragrant. Grind the toasted seeds in a mortar or spice mill, then put them in a bowl.

Add the paprika, red pepper, garlic, and salt. Stir in the olive oil and vinegar. The harissa will keep in the fridge for up to a week.   *makes about 1 cup*

Walnut Cigars

Exact proportions are not important in this dessert (this recipe yields about 20 cigars), and the nut filling can be altered to taste. I like to make the cigars with salted butter. Though the cigars are traditionally quite sweet, they're also delicious with barely any sugar. The quality of the nuts is crucial; look for fresh new-crop nuts. Supermarket nuts are often slightly rancid, so try a natural foods store or a Greek market. Toast them lightly, if you like, but fresh nuts don't really need it.

The cigars taste best if baked several hours before serving, or the day before. Serve and store at room temperature.

A bowl of new-crop walnuts in the shell would be another way to finish this meal, along with a bowl of tangerines or clementines. New walnuts have their own sweetness.

2 cups shelled walnuts

Sugar

Melted butter

Orange flower water

Organic almond extract

Cinnamon

Filo dough (from a package, thawed)

Honey

Pistachios (optional)

Chop the nuts coarsely. Add sugar to taste and 2 tablespoons melted butter. Sprinkle with orange flower water, a few drops of almond extract, and a little cinnamon. Add a few tablespoons of cold water and mix well.

For each cigar, take a sheet of filo dough, paint it with melted butter, and fold it in half lengthwise. Paint again. Place 2 to 3 tablespoons of the nut mixture in a strip along a short end. Roll loosely into a cigar shape.

Place the cigars side by side but not touching on a buttered baking sheet. Paint the tops generously with melted butter. Sprinkle with sugar.

Bake for 20 to 30 minutes in a 375°F oven, until golden and crisp. Drizzle generously with honey and sprinkle with chopped pistachios, if you like. Serve the cigars whole or cut them into wide slices.

In short, here is my advice: cook.

We are all cooks, each in our own fashion.

Cooking is learned in the same way as we learn to speak, write, act, dance. We observe, then we copy, then we interpret. As in learning a common language, we begin by imitating, then gradually develop our own way with words, our own style. Our interpretations differ even when we're using identical ingredients. Your version of these menus, your variations and adaptations, will make them your own.

Plant a few pots of herbs to grow on your windowsill. Go to the market. Talk to a farmer. Spend a little time in the kitchen. Set the table, gather your friends, and eat hearty.

ACKNOWLEDGMENTS

My sincere thanks to the following people:

To Christopher Hirsheimer for brilliant photography, astuteness, and panavision. To Melissa Hamilton for trout fishing and luminosity. To Dorothy Kalins for saving me from myself, and for wisdom beyond words.

To all the folks at Artisan, especially Ann Bramson, for their support, warmth, and incredible kindness: Sigi Nacson, Trent Duffy, Nancy Murray, and Judith Sutton. Thanks for your knowledgeable guidance. Thanks to Jan Derevjanik for a stunning design. Thanks to Barbara Tanis for a beautiful cover. To Katherine Cowles, agent and friend. For editorial support and help keeping the book alive, I thank Joan Simon, Fritz Streiff, Lynn Larsen, and Harriet Bell.

To Alice Waters and the entire staff at Chez Panisse, as well as to the convoluted and extended "family" of Panisse, I am forever indebted.

Thanks to chef Jean-Pierre Moullé for friendship and generosity and to Denise Lurton Moullé for rare insights into clafoutis, among other things.

Thanks to Bob Cannard, Charlene Nicholson Cannard, Bill Fujimoto, Paul Johnson, and the Chino family.

For major work on recipes and for steadfast friendship and help in the kitchen, thanks to Joe Evans and Nico Monday.

For additional recipe testing thanks to Oliver Schwaner-Albright, Diane Villani, Jeff Bretl, and Dottie Folley.

For sanctuary while writing, I thank Hugh Hamrick and David Sedaris, Milton Estes, Susan Rothenberg, and Bruce Nauman.

For being the best cooking and dining pals, I thank Tony Oltranti, Bob Carrau, Sue Murphy, Peggy Knickerbocker, Alta Tingle, Niloufer Ichaporia King, David King, Russell Moore, Allison Hopelain, Gilbert Pilgram, Richard Gilbert, Davia Nelson, Michael Wild, Jill Wild, Angelo Garro, Steven Barclay, Garth Bixler, Jérôme Waag, Kenny Parker, Caroline Gordon, Johanna Hill, Michael Sullivan, Sylvie Sullivan, Ernestine Kimbro, Lorin Leith, Otis Holt, Kate Coleman, Kevin West, Chris Galvin, Joe Guth, Katharine Kagel, Dan Welch, Deborah Madison, Patrick McFarland, Brian Knox, Jody Kent-Apple, Elizabeth Berry Sebastian, Andrew Sebastian, and Laura Calder.

For Italian expertise and inspiration, thanks to Stephen Singer, John Meis, Nancy Jenkins, Dario Cecchini, and Faith Willinger. For hospitality in Argentina, thanks to Fernando Trocca, Ignacio Mattos, and Juliana Lopez-May. In France, *merci infiniment* to Lulu Peyraud, Martine Labro, Claude Labro, Camille Labro, and Nathalie Waag. For her generosity and welcome in Mexico, thanks to Patricia Quintana. In Morocco, thanks to Mustapha Benzine and his family for extraordinary feasting and graciousness.

Thanks to my family: my sisters Barbara and Judith, my uncle Donald and aunt Ruth, my aunt Dottie (who has the recipe for the mythic Pineapple Blitz Torte), and in loving memory of my parents.

For everything else and everything in between, thanks to Randal Breski.

INDEX